Networl
Beginners

Easy Guide to Learn Basic/Advanced Computer Network, Hardware, Wireless, and Cabling. LTE, Internet, and Cyber Security

By Dylan Mach

Table of Contents

4

Introduction

Congratulations on downloading Networking for Beginners, and thank you for doing so. The world is becoming digital, and everyone has to keep up with the constant emerging technologies. However, you can't involve in any type of technology without understanding the basics at first. That is, you have to initially learn the principles of different computer components before sinking deeper into complex activities such as computer programming and more.

The following chapters will discuss all you need to know about networking in the computing world essential for those who are venturing into the industry. Some may have limited knowledge about networking, but you are likely to become a pro soon when using this guide. Therefore, you will learn about different protocols used in networking as well as interconnection and the internet, among others. There are fundamental concepts in networking and may also include other forms of operations related to computer networks.

That said, you will learn about computer networking and understand how the modern telecommunication network facilitates the sharing of resources among machines. Networking is a fundamental field of computer study which allows for computers to become interconnected globally. Also, you will learn about machine learning as a form of algorithms and statistical methods of how machines acquire an ability to perform a given task. Machine learning is a broad topic but essential for beginners, especially when they want to learn about how computers are capable of making decisions on situations like humans.

There are plenty of books on this subject on the market, thanks again for choosing this one! Every effort was made to ensure it is full of as much useful information as possible. Please enjoy!

Chapter 1:

Introduction to Machine Learning and Computer Networking

Machine learning and computer networking is both an essential field of study in computing but accompany different concepts. That is, they are topics that represent a similar study area on the contrary cover various sections of computer systems. In this case, machine learning entails computer algorithms and statistical models which facilitate the process of machine learning on data fed, the identity of suitable patterns, and the selection of the most favorable outcome. On the other hand, computer networking deals with the connections and interconnection of different computers globally, therefore, enabling data sharing, resource management, and user applications.

Computer Networking

Computer networking is the computing knowledge of studying and analyzing the communications techniques of computing devices or systems connected or interconnected together to exchange information or resources. A computer network is therefore defined as a group of computers allied together to communicate and share data and resources. Networking in computers solely depends on theoretical and practical applications of computer engineering, sciences, and telecommunication and information technologies. As to build computer networking between machines, an individual is required to have a router, network card, and specific protocols.

History of Computer Networks

Computer networking began during the rise of computers in the 1950s but utilized closed network systems used by the military. Unlike the modern networking systems, the late 1950s saw the use of military radars, which transitioned into MOS transistors consisting of transceivers, routers telecommunication circuits, and base station modules. Different developers proposed various forms of computer networking, including the introduction of a telephone switch in 1965 by the Western Electric. The first critical progress of

10

computer networks began in the 1970s, which saw multiple modifications of devices used today to promote networking.

One of them includes the Xerox PARC, which refers to the use of Ethernet, the X.25 used expanding IP network coverage and the creation of a host. From the supply of 50kb/s circuit in 1969 to the current 10mb/s to 100mb/s, the networking industry has undergone significant changes. However, the improvement is predicted to increase in the future, seeing the fastest modes of networks emerge, therefore building the computer networking sector. Besides, the higher speeds of the system have already been experienced with 2018. And this is because of the introduction of rates of up to 400 GB/s through the use of Ethernet fiber cables.

Components of Computer Networking

Routers

A router is the most common network device which forwards data packets in computer networks with a primary function of directing traffic on the internet. The packets such as web pages are transmitted from one router to another comprising of an internetwork while waiting to reach a desirable node destination. Routers are commonly used in homes and small networks and perform using network cables rather than installed drivers and connected to the computers by use of USBs or specific wires.

Routers may either be wireless or consist of cables linked by ports to allow for devices to connect to the internet. They usually linked to the modem, for instance, fiber and DSL, or WAN ports via network cables to facilitate the connection. Based on your desirable network link, your network speed will vary, with some regulating the rate you receive per individual router. Besides, routers may follow specific IP addresses depending on the internet connection, with the private addresses being the primary gateway default one for different devices in the network. Multiple links to one router, including both wireless and wired devices, enable each one to communicate freely, such as the sharing of a printer.

Network Interface Card

A network card is an electronic device that connects one computer to a network, usually to a Local Area Network (LAN). Most modern computers have an embedded network interface card in the motherboard instead of having an external chip to connect a network. These cards are critical when the computer exchanges data with the computer network using a given protocol such as CSMA/CD. Previous versions of network cards used included protocols such as ARCNET incorporated in 1977, but today most computers use Ethernet. The use of Ethernet network cards has been the most common with the revolution of computer networking being witnessed each year.

Internet speeds often vary on network interface cards based on the protocol standards supported. The previous Ethernet cards supported up to 10mb/s with the current adapters supporting from 100mb/s up to 1000mb/s. Network cards do not necessarily support wireless connections, but routers also contain these cards, which determines the speeds for a given computer network. The same has been projected to increase in the near future with the use of Ethernet network cards. In this case, speeds are to grow in the coming years, with rates tripling the current figure. This is attributed to the expansion of usage of computer networking across different platforms, both in small enterprises to commercial use over the years.

Protocols

Computer networking also comprises connection protocols that consist of rules for two or more systems to exchange data. Other than regulations, protocols also include syntaxes, communications synchronization, and semantics, as well as error recovery techniques, use in both hardware and software of computer connection. In other words, protocols are a set of rules which connect the server to the routers regardless of the variations in infrastructure, designs, and standards. As to exchange information, both parties much adhere to accept the protocols built in the hardware, software, or both.

Networking protocols usually accompany similar languages for the devices to facilitate the interaction between the two computers in the exchange of information. Network protocols typically utilize the Open Systems Interconnection (OSI) model used to break down the complicated process to readily defined functions and operations. There are multiple protocols used in computer networking, Transmission Control Protocol (TCP), User Datagram Protocol (UDP), Internal Protocol (IP), Hypertext Transfer Protocol (HTTP), and File Transfer Protocol (FTP), among others.

Types of Computer Networks

Local Area Network (LAN)

Local Area Network, commonly referred by its abbreviation, LAN, is a group of computer systems using and sharing a particular internet connection within a given small area such as the office or residential building. The LAN connection is usually through a communication medium, for instance, coaxial cables used by two or more personal computers. This type of computer network is often cheaper than other types and accessed by those within the area and uses hardware such as adapters and Ethernet cables. Transfer of data is commonly extremely fast with considerably higher security. The connection only supports those within the area, and anyone outside tends to lack the transmission of information.

Personal Area Network (PAN)

This is a type of private network arranged within an area of 10 meters and often for personal use with devices within a given range. Personal Area Network was first researched and introduced by Thomas Zimmerman, who established that an individual could create a connection with communities with devices within 30 feet. Both wired and wireless PAN can be used in this type to connect to devices around the source. The source more so may generate from media players, laptops, and mobile phones. Wireless is usually connected using hotspots, Bluetooth, and Wi-Fi connected to devices within a given range. Wired PAN is connected by USB cables to facilitate the connection of a given network. Personal Area Network always moves with the person and can include offline systems and uses to connect devices using a VPN in small home networks.

Metropolitan Area Network (MAN)

Metropolitan Area Network is computer network which covers a wide range of a geographical area by interconnecting several LAN connections. This type of computer network is often used by government agencies to connect to different federal facilities as well as their citizens and private organizations. Some of the protocols in MAN include ISDN, Frame Relay, and OC-3, among others, which connect to different LANs through an exchange line. This form of a computer network is used in larger areas than that of LAN and such as airline reservations, military communication, colleges, and between banks.

Wide Area Network (WAN)

Wide Area Network is extended computer network coverage over a large geographical area such as between states or countries. It is quite extensive than LAN and WAN and not limited to one domain but covers an entirely larger area by use of satellite connections or fiber optic cables. WAN is the largest of all computer networks in the world and used in businesses, government operations, and educational purposes. Some of the advantages of WAN include centralized data, fast message transfer, coverage of a full geographical area, higher bandwidth, and supports global businesses. On the other hand, WAN can become disadvantageous in the case of a security breach; it demands a firewall and rigid antiviruses, expensive setup costs, and difficulty fixing problems due to its more comprehensive coverage.

Machine Learning

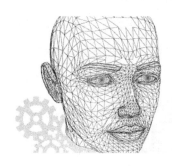

As mentioned, machine learning is the method of data analysis by computers where algorithms and statistical models play a role for machines to learn from data and patterns and then make decisions without human interactions. Since its incorporation in the late 1950s, machine learning has gained popularity and become a vast topic in computing. It is a branch of artificial intelligence enabling computers to provide analytical information about the future with limited human interaction. Machine learning can, therefore, be learned in different ways depending on the part an individual chooses to follow.

The idea of machine learning takes the form of the human brain, including the neurons and how they facilitate the assimilation of information, thinking, and making decisions. When the concept was first introduced to computers in 1943, it focused on neural networks where machines became capable of learning on their own, depending on the information fed. That is, machines were able to observe, learn, understand, analyze, and make decisions based on the event without depending on individual instructions. However, the slow development of computers at the time increased the challenges of machine learning when compared to the current days.

As humans have the ability to develop and expand their knowledge about an event or something they first or learn, the same technique, therefore, facilitate machine learning. Besides, humans depend on networks of neurons in the brain, and computers utilize a similar pattern. As such, machine work with the same technique, therefore, can manage to make decisions and conclusions without any human interaction. However, the decisions made by computers are widely based on mathematical and algorithms that have expanded to make them predict the outcome of things that haven't happened yet. Currently, different methods have been used, therefore enabling computers to learn specific information; therefore, be able to provide predictions, conclusions, and decisions based on specific datasets.

Machine Learning Vs. Computer Programming

Machine learning has been widely confused with computer language programming, which in this case, has significant dissimilarities. As defined, machine learning is all about the machine receiving specific data sets, selecting the most reliable algorithm, learn and determine the outcome without any human interaction. It, therefore, has limited interaction, especially when analysis the information, learning, and making positive outcomes. On the contrary, computer programming requires human interaction who first selects datasets to use and writing them in the machine. The codes are then executed to create a specific program, which is, therefore, the outcome. In programming, machines rarely learn but generated results based on the instructions provided by humans.

General Steps in Machine Learning

Collection and Preparation of Data

Humans can never learn and have knowledge about something without having an interaction or understanding the basics. Similarly, machines face a similar challenge, as they also have to gain access to relevant information about something before learning in detail about it. As such, the first step in machine learning is to collect the necessary data and prepare it in a way that fits a given criterion. The collection comprises of gaining access to specific details about a given element and begin having an understanding about it. The computer then prepares the system to internalize the information before providing the needed knowledge.

Selection of Instructing Models

Humans also undergo trial and error in order to come up with an effective solution to a problem at hand. Machine learning also creates multiple models based on the instructions fed to provide the most suitable model, which can solve a given problem. In this case, the computer uses algorithms which have been modified differently since their incorporation. Over the years, more models have been developed with the objective of making machines more specific in some regions of specialization. In this step, computers, therefore, select the most desirable model that best suits a given dataset and train itself through learning more about the information at hand. This ensures that the information fed and the outcomes are more likely to become beneficial and provide the intended solution.

Evaluation of Models

The last step is now to put the model selected into practice by trying to figure out if the model which enables the machine to learn and make decisions without human interaction. Machines readily learn from the information fed and create patterns and work like how we behave on newfound knowledge in our minds. That is, when supplied with well-tested details, the machine will offer excellent results with inadequate tests leading to vogue and harmful outcomes. In this step, you need to feed the computer with the relevant models and data which provide an algorithm where the machine will follow and deliver effective results. Therefore, test the data and model, which provides certainty of delivering exceptional results.

Types of Machine Learning Algorithms

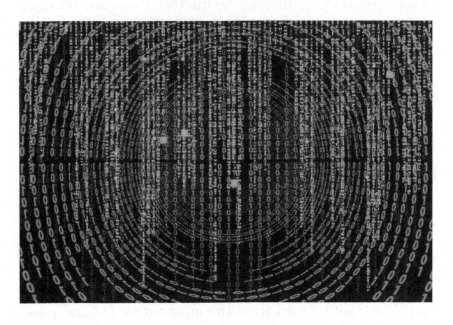

Supervised Algorithms

As mentioned, machine learning comprises of multiple types depending on how the data fed is to yield the outcome. One of the models is the supervised algorithm, where the datasets undergo a given set of parameters, which in turn determine the outcome. The machine initially specifies the data into labels as well as the training data included. In this case, the data is initially tested to ascertain its outcome, therefore, controlling the outcome. This type of algorithm usually has a manageable as a result is generally intended. Supervised algorithms are further subdivided into classification and regression algorithms.

The classification algorithm uses the K-Nearest Neighbor classification algorithm, which is responsible for sorting data into individual labels. The data is classified depending on the similarities between variables or the information inputted in the machine. On the other hand, regression algorithms focus on mathematical relationships and the dependency of variables. That is, it provides an immediate analysis of numerical datasets with similarities essential for predicting the future. The regression algorithm includes two forms depending on the information fed, linear, and logistic regression models.

Unsupervised Algorithms

This is the opposite of supervised algorithms and consists of unlabeled datasets, which in most cases, the results are undetermined. The unsupervised algorithm is classified into K-means clustering, recurrent, and artificial neural network. The artificial neural networks resemble the brain neurons, which are connected and interconnected to enhance learning, thinking, and making decisions without any interventions. K-means clustering entails the grouping of similar data into clusters to promote learning in machines. While recurrent neural networks use the memory in the nodes of computer neurons to analyze sequential information for the benefit of encouraging decision making in devices.

Reinforcement Algorithms

Reinforcement algorithms are where the machines determine specific information is the datasets within particular contexts. As one of the types of machine learning algorithms, reinforcement models are the most beneficial as learning of specific datasets leads to the maximization of the outcome. However, if the wrong dataset is fed into the machine, it may result in extensive punishments or other related dangers. But when using the right parameters, the device will make the needed corrections and yield positive results. Besides, this type of machine learning algorithm enables you to quickly make corrections, modifications, or change the outcome if you feel it may become undesirable in the future.

Applications of Machine Learning

Since the introduction of machine learning in the computing industry, different sectors have benefited significantly in their operations. More so, it has popularity between developers as well as other users, making it applicable in different areas. In this case, the applications of machine learning range from small scale technological businesses to commercial use. One of the common areas includes social media such as Facebook and Twitter used for sentimental analysis, spam filtering, facial recognition, among others. It is also applied in the e-commerce sector to display items that are mostly searched by specific clients. Machine learning is also used in areas such as transport, health, trading, visual assistance, and financial services.

Chapter 2:

Properties of a Computer Network

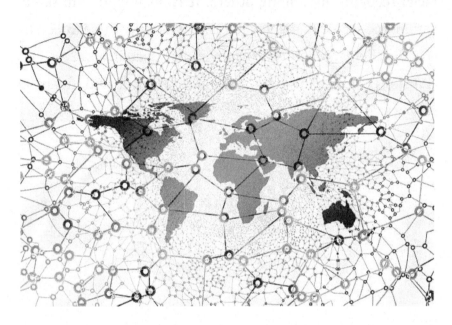

A computer network is defined as a digital telecommunications network that allows resources to be shared between nodes. A telecommunication network is a number of terminal nodes having connected links that would enable telecommunication between some terminals. Transmission links in the network act as a connection between nodes. Telecommunications network allows for interactions and transfer of information over long distances.

Computer network involves a connection between computer

systems and computer hardware devices via communication channels. The communication channels enable communication and sharing of resources amongst many users. The connections between nodes are referred to as data links. The establishment of the data links is usually from cable media, including optic cables or wires, and wireless media, including Wi-Fi.

Network nodes are the network computer devices originating, routing, and terminating the data. Typically, the nodes are identified through network addresses, and generally include elements such as phones, personal computers, networking hardware, and servers. The devices are easily networked together as long as one of the tools has the ability to exchange information with the other devices. The devices can either have or not have a direct connection with each other.

A wide range of services and applications are supported by computer networks. Some of them include accessing the digital audio, digital video, World Wide Web, the common use of storage servers, and applications, fax machines, and printers. It may also include the use of instant messaging and e-mail applications. Computer networks differ from other telecommunication networks because of the transmitting mediums they use in carrying their signals, protocols used in organizing network traffic, size of the networks, the mechanism in controlling traffic, organizational intent, and topology. One of the most common computer networks is the Internet.

Computer networks have been in existence since the late 1950s. During this time, computer networks involved the Semi-Automatic Ground Environment. The SAGE was a radar system used by the U.S military. A reorganization was later planned in 1959. It was based on the network of the OGAS, which were computing center networks. The MOS transistor was also invented in 1959 at Bell Labs by Dawon Kahng, and Mohamed Atalla. The conductor was one of the significant steps towards computer network communication infrastructure. It included base station modules, routers, memory chips, telecommunication circuits, microprocessors, transceivers, and RF power amplifiers.

SABRE a system in the commercial airline reservation, managed to go online with two mainframes that were connected together in 1960. The intergalactic computer network was later invented in 1963. It allowed for general communications amongst many computer users. In 1964, some researchers came up with an operation where a computer was used in routing and managing connections between telephones.

The concept of packet switching was developed all through the

1960s. It allowed for information to be transferred among computers through a network. A telephone was also used in implementing the precise control of computers. A paper was later published on Wide Area Network that allowed computers to share time.

French CYCLADES hosts were developed by 1973. The hosts had the responsibility to deliver data instead of centralizing services on the network reliably. A formal memo was written in the same year with a description of Ethernet. Ethernet is one of the most common networking systems used in the world today. Robert Metcalfe worked from 1979 in a bid to make Ethernet open standard. Ethernet continued being upgraded to a 10Mbit/s protocol in the 1980s.

By 1995, Ethernet was supporting gigabit speeds. It has the capability of having a transmission speed of up to 400Gbit/s as recorded in 2018. The continued use of Ethernet results from its capacity to adapt and to scale easily.

Properties of Computer Network

Computer networking is considered a subdivision of electronics engineering, computer engineering, computer science, electrical engineering, information technology, or telecommunications. This is because the practical and theoretical computer networking relies on have close relations to the fields.

Computer networks allow for efficient interpersonal communication between users. They can effectively communicate through video telephone calls, telephone, online chats, instant messaging, video conferencing, and e-mails. It also allows for network and computing resources sharing among users. Accessing and using resources is made easier through the devices on the network. Users can, for instance, share printers and storage devices together. Data, files, and other forms of information can also be shared effectively using computer networks.

Uses of Computer Networks

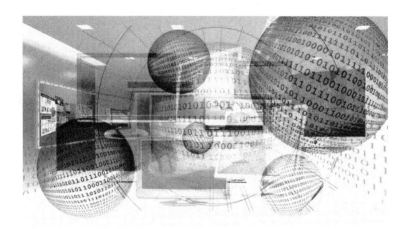

If it were not beneficial, people would not have considered creating a connection between computers through a network. There are numerous users of computer networks in the world today. They are used to benefit both individuals and companies in the long run.

Use in Business Applications

• Resource Sharing

The main goal of computer networks is ensuring the anything

about a business is available to all those who take part. Computer networks allow for this access by making all equipment, data, and programs available to any person using the network. Any user can access the use of the computer network regardless of their physical location.

• Server-Client Model

In such a model, the information about a business is stored on servers, which are powerful computers. The servers are housed centrally, and a system administrator is used to maintain them. The business employees usually have clients, which are simple machines on their office desks. The server-client model allows for easier access to remote data and information by these employees.

• Communication-Medium

Employees in a business setting need to communicate on various issues affecting business operations regularly. Computer networks, therefore, offer a powerful medium for communication among the employees. Almost all companies have several computers with logged-in e-mails. Employees use these computers when on great deals of communicating on a daily basis. An employer can send a message, and everyone engaging in the business operations can easily receive it.

- ## eCommerce

One of the most significant targets of every business is the ability to do business with potential customers through the Internet. In the modern world, most customers prefer doing their shopping from home. Numerous ventures such as music vendors, books, and food stores have considered using computer networks to meet the needs of their customers.

- ## High Reliability because of Alternative Sources of Data

Computer networks provide higher reliability by providing numerous sources of data. This means that general files can be copied on many machines. When one of the machines is not available, another one can be used to access the same information. The concept of Reliability is significant in banking, military, nuclear reactor safety, and military. This is because such sectors require consistent operations, even when there are hardware and software failures.

- ## Money-Saving

Computer networking is a significant concept of the financial aspect for many companies and businesses. This is because it saves a considerable amount of money. Computer networks provide an option for using personal computers rather than mainframe computers that are quite expensive. Companies can effectively use the peer to peer model by networking all personal computers together. Everyone in the organization can access the network for many purposes, such as communication. The domain model offered by computer networks can help to provide security to the operations of an organization. Clients involved in the organization can access data and communicate with the organization through the server.

- ## Computer Networks: Home Applications

Home users also consider using computer networks for various reasons. Some of these include:

Accessing remote information- People connect their devices for easier access to useful information.

Person-to- person communication- This communication includes sending e-mails or other forms of communication. Remote users are able to communicate with other people easily. They are able to see and hear from other people who are away from them without delays. Video-conferencing is one of the most popular person-to-person communication, is used in remote schools, or receiving medical opinions from medical practitioners who are distant. People also consider using computer networks to access information posted by worldwide newsgroups easily. Through these networks, people easily give their feedbacks regardless of their physical location.

Interactive Entertainment- Computer networks allow for easier access to videos on demand, multi-person simulation games, and participation of people in live television programs such as discussions, and quizzes. It is through these networks that people can feel the entertainment from the comfort of their homes. People also use computer networks as home applications for electronic commerce.

Computer Networks: Mobile Users

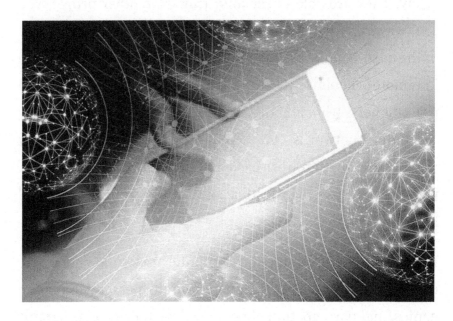

Mobile computers include personal digital assistants and notebooks. They are one of the segments in the computer industry growing at a very rapid rate. Owners of mobile computers usually possess desktop computers in their offices and prefer connecting them to their portable computers based at home. Computer networks allow for wireless connection to these devices, even when in an airplane or a car. One main reason why people connect to these mobile computers is to allow them to receive telephone calls and messages, send faxes, e-mails, access remote files, and surf through the web.

People are able to do all this from any location away from their office.

More Information on Types of Computer Networks

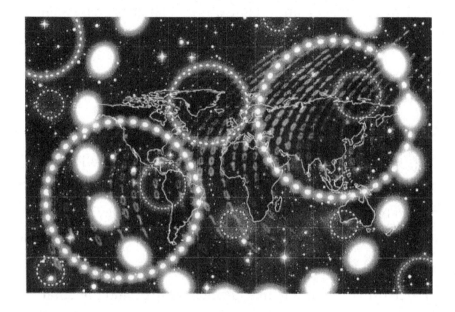

Computer networks are basically used for numerous tasks in the world today. Some of the tasks include downloading attachments and printing documents. This is done by referring to several devices within a room and spreading them across the entire world. This can be defined based on their purpose or their size. Below are some of the common types of computer networks.

- ## **Personal Area Network (PAN)**

A personal area network is the most basic and smallest type of computer network. It is comprised of a computer(s), phones, tablets, printers, and a wireless modem. PAN revolves around a single person within a building. The networks are commonly used in residences and small offices. Their management is controlled by one organization or person from one device.

- ## **Local Area Network (LAN)**

Local area networks are popularly discussed by people in the world today. They are one of the most original, simplest, and common types of computer networks. They are used in connecting together several computers and devices of low voltage. The devices are usually within short distances, such as different rooms within a building or several buildings close to each other. They help in sharing resources and information among the connected devices. LAN computer networks are commonly used by enterprises. They are easily manageable and maintainable.

- ## **Wireless Local Area Network (WLAN)**

WLAN networks function in a similar way as the LAN

networks. The networks use wireless network technology. Some of them include Wi-Fi. WLAN networks do not require devices to have physical cables when connecting to it.

• Campus Area Network

Campus area networks are quite larger than Local area networks but smaller than the metropolitan area networks. CANs are commonly used in small businesses, universities, colleges, and large school districts. Campus area networks are spread across a number of buildings that are closer to each other. They allow any user in the different buildings to connect and share resources.

• Metropolitan Area Networks

Metropolitan networks are larger than the local area networks but smaller than the wide-area networks. They include the elements of both types of computer networks. MANS computer networks can spread on a whole geographical area such as a city or a town. The ownership and management of the computer network is usually under one company, such as a local council or by a single person such as the owner of a particular company.

- # Wide Area Network

Wide area network is quite complex as compared to the local area network. WANs computer networks easily create connections with computers in wide distant locations. Low voltage devices, as well as computers, create a remote connection with each other. They do this through a single large network allowing communication even longer distances. WAN computer networks have different categories, with the Internet being the most basic type. The Internet allows for the connection of computers all over the globe. Numerous public and administration entities typically own WAN computer networks. This is possible due to its wider reach.

- # Storage-Area Network (SAN)

SAN computer networks are of high-speed and significantly dedicated. They create connections between shared sources of storage devices and various servers. SAN networks do not rely on WAN and LAN. The computer networks typically removed the storage devices from the computer networks and put them on their high-performance networks. The computer networks are accessible similarly to drives attached to servers. Some of the types of Storage Area Networks include, unified SANs, and converged virtual SANs.

- ## System-Area Network

This type of computer network is quite new and is also abbreviated as SANs. The computer networks are basically used in defining relative local networks. The networks are designed high-speed connections in applications involving servers, processors, as well as storage area networks. Computers are connected to this type of network operating as single systems and offer very rapid speeds.

- ## Passive Optical Local Area Network (POLAN)

POLAN computer networks are used as a substitute for traditional switch-based Ethernet LANs. The technology used in POLAN computer networks is added to structured cabling. The reason behind the integration is overcoming concerns on the support of traditional network applications, and Ethernet protocols. Optical splitters are used in POLAN to enhance the splitting of optical signals from a single strand. Single-mode-mode optical fibers are transformed into numerous signals that serve devices and users.

- ## Enterprise Private Network (EPN)

Enterprise private Networks are owned by businesses that

typically build them. Businesses prefer this type of computer networks as a way of securing the connection between various locations that share the network.

- ## Virtual Private Network (VPN)

The extension of a private network all over the Internet is made possible by the use of Virtual Private Network. Sending and receiving information and data between connected devices is also made possible by the VPNs computer networks. The process is also possible when users are using devices that are not directly connected. Access to remote private networks is also made possible through a connection referred to as point-to-point.

Basic Elements of Computer Networks

Computer Networks comprise of systems through which a connection is created between numerous nodes. The links help them to share resources and information. Computer network elements are the fundamental objects used in computer networks. Basically, there are four significant elements of computer networking. These include computers, transmission medium, protocols, and network software. For a computer network to successfully function, all the elements have to work in coordination.

• Computers

Computers are digital devices that can accept input in the form of data, process it through the use of data structures, and predefined algorithms, performing tasks in the form of output. The process can be defined as transforming raw data into useful information. The output provided includes performing several physical tasks as well as storing data, transforming it as well as retrieving it when in need. The network is created by computers to allow for leveraging of distributed models of programming and interchanging data to allow for equivalent processing.

• Transmission Medium

The transmission medium is the path through which users send data from one place to a new place. When representing data, computers and telecommunication devices make use of signals. The transmission of the signals from one device to the other is generally through electromagnetic energy. They are transmitted through air, vacuums, and different modes from the sender to the receiver. There are two types of transmission mediums. The Guided or Wired transmission mediums include optical fiber cables, twisted pair cable, and coaxial cables. The Unguided or Wireless transmission mediums include infrared, radio waves, and microwaves.

• **Protocols**

Protocols are the defined conventions and rules guiding communication between computer network devices. Computer network protocols consist of device mechanisms used in identifying and making connections between each other. Formality rules are used in specifying the method of packaging data in the form of received and sent messages. There are three types of protocols. The internet protocols, wireless network protocols, and network routing protocols.

Internet protocols are the rules set to govern the format of sending data through the Internet or over another network. They are the standards used to address and route data on the Internet. The internet protocols deliver packets from the host to a destination host entirely depending on the addresses on the headers of the packages. Wireless network protocols involve a collection of wireless devices and laptops engaging in communication through radio waves. Computer network routing protocols, on the other hand, are used in specifying methods through which routers are communicating with each other. They do this through the distribution of information, enabling them to choose routes among nodes within computer networks. Routing algorithms are used when determining particular routes of choice. Computer network routing protocols are capable of adjusting dynamically to evolving conditions, including disabled computers, and data lines.

• **Network Software**

Computer networks use network software as foundation elements for all networks. Network software assists administrators in deploying, managing, and monitoring any network. Numerous traditional networks consist of special hardware, including switches and routers that integrate networking software in the combination. Networking software consists of a wide range of software applied in designing, implementing, operating, and monitoring computer networks. Most traditional computer networks were based on hardware but embedded in the software. Defined Networking, that was software like emerged and led to the separation of software from hardware. This separation made network software much adaptable to the evolving nature of computer networks.

Choosing a Suitable Computer Network

There are factors that one should consider when selecting a computer network type for an organization. These factors include:

The Organization- One should consider finding out the sector of the economy that the organization operates, what the organization is providing, the number of people employed in the organization, as well as the jobs they are working on.

Existing Systems- It is essential to check on the existing computer network components, the network operating system, network architecture, transmission medium, and topology.

Number of Users- Prior to choosing a computer network for an organization, it is crucial to check on the number of users. This is because organizations tend to have users working on separate as well as shared workstations.

Functionality- Consider checking on tasks undertaken by the network users as well as software applications being used in carrying out the tasks.

Budget- Consider choosing a computer network operator that

is within your budget. This helps to guarantee successful implementation and maintenance of the network.

Chapter 3:

Easy Guide to Learn

Basic Computer

Network

This article discusses the basic components of computer networking and the easy ways you can learn them. It also extensively discusses the advanced features of computer networking as well as how you can learn and apply them. Read on to find out!

Computer Networking has been in existence for quite some time now, and with time, technology has become quicker and more affordable. These networks are a build-up of various devices and components, including computers, routers, and switches, which are linked together by wireless signals or cables. Learning how these networks and connections are assembled is very essential in creating a network that can be used for many purposes.

In the quest of breaking this giant of a topic down, let us start by discussing the essential components of any computer network.

The Important Components of a Computer Network

This is the first thing you need to look at when learning computer networks. Any computer network is made up of four very important components: Media, Networking Devices, Protocols, and End Devices. Let us discuss each of these essential components.

• The End Devices

This is a kind of device that either sends or receives a set of data or information within a particular network. End devices can be laptops, smartphones, PC, or any kind of machine with the capabilities of receiving or sending the set of data within the connected network. For your information, you will need a minimum of two devices to build a network.

There are two types of end devices: client end devices and the server end devices. The server end device is responsible for providing service or data. On the other hand, the client end device is one which is responsible for receiving the data offered from the former (the server end device).

- ## The Media

This is a very important component of the computer network that provides connectivity and linkage for the end devices. End devices are not able to exchange services or data unless they are connected through any kind of media. As of today, there exist mainly two categories or types of media: the wired media and the wireless media.

Radio signals are mainly applied in transferring data and information between the end devices when using Wireless Media. In wired media, however, cables are used instead.

The above-mentioned types of media are further subdivided into various subtypes depending on factors like the data transfer speed, length, frequency band, among others. The subtypes are commonly referred to as media standards. The media standards that are popular and widely applied are the IEEE802.11 (also known as Wi-Fi standards) and the Ethernet.

The two media standards play different essential roles. The Ethernet is responsible for defining standards for wired media while the IEEE802.11 plays a role in defining standards for wireless media.

• **The Protocols**

Just like the previous two, this is a very important component of a computer network. Protocols are responsible for the communication between the involved end devices; they could be two or more. A protocol is defined as a group of rules that highlights and specifies the standards for a specific or all the stages of communication.

Below are some known roles played by protocols.

- o Starting and ending the communication process.
- o Doing Encryption and compressions before transferring any data.
- o Packaging data in such a format that it is able to travel within a network.
- o Establishing and providing logical addresses

- o Carrying out error correction processes
- o Performing media authentication

Two popular models of networking describe the functionalities of most common protocols: TCP/IP model and the OSI reference model. These models categorize the entire process of communication into logical layers. They further explain how each protocol works in every layer, which enables the process of communication.

• **The Networking Device**

This is an essential component of computer networking that works in between the end devices. It is responsible for controlling the smooth flow of data. Depending on its functionality, networking devices are categorized into three different types; the forwarding device, the connecting device, and lastly, the securing device. Below, we discuss the functionality of each of the mentioned devices.

- o **Connecting Device:** It is responsible for connecting two or more types of protocols and media. In situations where two end devices are situated in different geographical networks or connected via a distinct type of media, they will require a connecting hatchet to carry out data exchange. This functionality can be provided through Multilayer and Router switch.

- **Securing Device**: This device is responsible for securing data from any unauthorized access. The securing device does security checks basing on the predefined rules whenever it receives a data packet. It then forwards it or rejects it based on the decision made. Some of the commonly known devices that perform these functions are NAT and Firewall.

- **Forwarding Device:** This is a device responsible for forwarding data. It has multiple sections and ports mainly used in connecting more two or more end devices in just one network. The two commonly known devices for these functions are Hub, Ethernet, and Bridge switches.

Having learned about the four essential components of a computer network, we next discuss other features that are much significance in computer networking.

Routers, switches, and wireless access points play a very significant role in computer networks. Below, discuss how this is done.

• Switches

These are the basic requirement for the majority of business networks. A switch, as most of us know, acts as controller linking printers, computers and servers within a computer network.

They enable the devices within a network to establish communication within themselves as wells as building a network commonly shared resources. Switches save a lot of money through resource allocation and sharing. They also increase the rate of productivity. There exist two commonly known types of switches in computer networking; managed switches and unmanaged switches.

An unmanaged type of switch is that which is able to work outside the box and can not be configured. The network equipment established at home specifically offers unmanaged switches. On the other hand, a managed switch is that which can be configured. It gives you the capability to adjust and monitor the progress of network traffic. It, therefore, gives you more control over the entire networking process.

• **Routers**

These are essential components that are responsible for connecting multiple sets of networks. They are also tasked with connecting the computers within a given network to a functioning Internet. They make it possible for all the networked devices or computers to share one Internet connection, which in the long run, saves you money.

Routers act as dispatchers. They analyze the data sent across a given network, find the quickest route data can travel and sends it that way.

They are able to link your business to the outside world, protect the vital information from threats, and even make decisions on the computers that are eligible to receive more attention over others.

Apart from the known networking roles they play, routers are equipped with a set of more features that make the networking process even easier and safer. Basing on the needs you have, for instance, you can buy a router with a virtual private network commonly known as VPN, a firewall, or the Internet Protocol, which is commonly known as IP.

• The Access Points

This is another essential aspect of a computer network that enables the devices to link to the network (a wireless network) without using cables. Wireless networks make it easier to invite fresh devices on online networks and give a flexible form of assistance to remote workers.

They act as amplifiers for your computer network. While routers provide bandwidth, the access point broadens the provided bandwidth in ways that networks are able to provide support to a good number of devices. These devices can then access the Internet from locations far away from where the router is located.

What you should know, however, is that the access points don't just extend the Wi-Fi reach. It also provides essential information about devices connected to the network; it also gives proactive safety measures and plays other critical functions.

Additionally, the access points can support various IEEE standards. Every standard, as we have discussed earlier, is an assortment that has been ratified over a period of time. Such standards run on a set of different frequencies, produce a different set of bandwidth and provide the help needed from a host of deferent channels.

• **Wireless Networks**

When creating a wireless network, you have the option to choose between four different types of deployment. Every form of deployment has characteristics that work better in various solution searching missions.

o **Cisco Mobility Express:** Cisco mobility is a simple, best performing wireless solution that is aimed at helping medium or small-sized companies. It is equipped with complete features of cisco that usually preconfigured the best practices of Cisco advance. The defaults created will enable the fast and effortless deployment of Wi-Fi that can operate in a few minutes. This is the most recommended module, especially for small computer networking businesses.

- ○ **The Centralized Deployment:** The commonly known type of computer networking system is centralized deployment. They are basically used in learning institutions where structures are located closer together. This kind of deployment involves a wireless network that eases upgrades and ensures the advanced functionality of wireless networks. The controllers of these devices are installed based on-premises and set up in mostly in a central location.

- ○ **The Converged Deployment:** This kind of deployment is mostly done in small proximity establishments like small campuses or branch offices. That provides a set of consistency in both wired and wireless connections. The convergent deployment redirects the wired and wireless connections on a single network and then carries out the double role of the switch and as the wifeless controller.

- o **The Cloud-Based Deployment:** This deployment method puts into use the cloud to run the devices dispatched on-site at different locations. This kind of solution needs a Cisco Meraki cloud-managed gadget that gives a full view of a computer network through visible dashboards.

The Classification of Computer Network

Having learned about the essential details of a computer network, it is time we discussed the classification of computer networks. This is a very important topic for anyone in quest of learning computer networking.

Computer networks are categorized based on various factors, namely: the geographical location, the relationship between devices, and the access types.

Let us look at each criterion and find out the credentials in detail.

Basing on Geographical Location

When using the geographical coverage criteria, the network device is subdivided into three different types: MAN, WAN, and LAN. The network spread in small, medium, and much wider geographical areas are referred to as the WAN, LAN, and MAN work networks in that order.

Based on the Access Type

When basing on allowing different users to have access to the network resources, the network can be grouped into three different types: Intranet, Extranet, and lastly, the Internet.

Intranet refers to any private network. In this kind of network, users from outside do not have access to provided network resources.

An extranet is almost similar to an intranet as it is a private network. In this network, however, external users are allowed access to a small portion of internet resources after proper scrutiny and authorization.

The Internet, on the other hand, is a public network. Any individual or user can have access to it provided they have devices that can access it.

Basing on Relationships between End Devices

In this criteria, the Internet is broken down into two sets: the clients/server network and the peer to peer network. In the peer to peer network, the available end devices all have fair, equal rights. In the client/server network, however, the decision on which client will receive what rights lie in the hands of the server.

Next, we look at the various types of computer networks. This is also a very important area where, as a person learning computer networking, you need to know.

Computer networks are categorized by their size. There are mainly four types of computer networks, namely; WAN (Wide Area Network), MAN(Metropolitan Area Network), PAN (Personal Area Network) and LAN (Local Area Network). Let us discuss each of these networks extensively and find out what they entail.

• Local Area Network (LAN)

LAN refers to a number of computers linked and connected to

one another within a small space like a house or office. The Local Area Network is mainly used in the connection of two or more computers via a communication channel such as the coaxial cable and the twisted pair. LAN is cheaper because it is constructed with affordable hardware, including Ethernet cables, network adapters as well as hubs. Data is transferred quicker in LAN than any other network. The Local Area Network gives more secure network options.

• The Personal Area Network (PAN)

This is a type of network that is arranged around an individual, to be more specific, within ten meters. PAN is mainly used in connecting computer devices that mainly for personal use. Thomas Zimmerman, a research scientist, first brought the idea of Personal Area Network. This kind of network can cover an area of up to 30 feet. You can use personal computers to develop this kind of network. Such kinds of computers are mobile phones, laptops, desktops, play stations, and media players.

As of today, there exist two categories of Personal Area Network: Wired Personal Area Network and the Wireless Personal Area Network. The wireless one is developed by the use of wireless innovations like Bluetooth and Wi-Fi. This is usually a low range network.

The wired network, on the other hand, is built by the use of USB cables.

• Examples of PAN

The Body Area Network: this is a kind of network that is moved along with a person. For instance, mobile networks are moved with an individual. Now suppose that the individual in possession of the mobile network establishes a connection and invites other devices to share the information and connection.

Offline Networks: This kind of network can be built when just at home. It is specially designed to connect and link different devices, namely computers, printers, and radio sets. You, however, need to note that the devices are not connected to the Internet.

The Small Home Office: This kind of network is mainly used to link and connect a number of elements to the internet connection and a cooperate link through a VPN.

- ## The Metropolitan Area Network (MAN)

MAN is a kind of network that can cover a large geographical area by joining a different kind of local area network to create a larger network. The metropolitan area network is mainly used in government organizations as well as private companies to connect citizens. In this kind of network, there are several local area networks connected via a telephone line. Some of the commonly used protocols in metropolitan area networks are ATM, Frame Relay ADSL, among others. MAN has a wide coverage and range compared to the local land network.

- ## Uses of MAN

It is used in establishing communication between financial institutions like banks within a city.

MAN can be applied in the reservation of airlines.

Additionally, a metropolitan area network is used in learning institutions that are located within a city. It is also used in the creation of communication modules in the military.

- ## **The Wide Area Network (WAN)**

WAN is a kind of network that covers very large geographical locations and regions like countries or States. WAN is very big compared to the local area network. It is not pinned down to a single location but rather can be distributed over large areas through fiber optic cables or satellite links. For your information, the Internet is one of the best forms of WAN. The Wide Area Network is largely used in fields of education, business, and government.

- ## **Examples of WAN**

The mobile broadband: in this kind of network, the 4G network is popularly used across a country.

Last Mile Internet: This is the situation where a telecommunication company provides internet services to users in different locations by connecting their residences with fiber optic internet.

The Private Network: Banks provide a set of private networks that can connect up to forty-four offices. The private network is build using telephone lines usually provided by telecom companies in charge.

- **Advantages of WAN**

  Highlighted below are some of the advantages of WAN.

  The geographical coverage: WAN covers a larger geographical location than any other network. For instance, if a branch of a certain office is located in a different town or city, you can be connected to it through the Wide Area Network. The Internet gives a leeway through which you can be able to connect with a branch located in a different location.

  It offers Centralized Data: Data is centralized in Wide area networks. You, therefore, don't require to have emails or other back up systems.

  Wide Area Network has provided an updated file. Various software organizations have work done on live servers. This means that programmers are able to access updated files within a matter of seconds.

  WAN networks provide for the exchange of Messages where they are transferred in a fast way. You can see how this is applied in real life through web apps like Facebook and Skype, which allow you to communicate with loved ones.

WAN enables the sharing of resources and software: You are allowed to share software and a host of other resources like RAM when using the wide-area network.

Additionally, WAN enables you to do business in large, global regions.

Lastly, the wide-area network has higher bandwidth. It occurs If you decide to use lines that have been leased for your company when WAN gives you the highest bandwidth. Higher bandwidth is capable of increasing the rate of data transfer, which in return improves the productivity of your organization.

The Internetwork

This can be defined as a number of computer networks, WAN, or LANs that are linked using devices and configured by the basic addressing machine. The process of doing all this is referred to as interconnection. Having interconnections between commercial, public, and private computer networks can also be referred to as internetworking. Mostly, internetworking uses internet protocol. Open System Interconnection (OSI) is the model of reference used in internetworking.

Chapter 4:

What Are the Basic Cybersecurity Fundamentals?

Cybersecurity is a popular name in the internet and other technological advancement areas. It has got many concerns recently due to the increased cyber threats and attacks. Simply because; more systems are being targeted using more sophisticated strategies in assaults. It is a menace that has an impact on small-scale and large-scale businesses, individuals, organizations, schools, workplaces, and so on. It is with great importance that we all have to understand cybersecurity and what measures we can invent to solve any threats and attacks.

Recently, there has been growth in the use of mobile banking, social networking, and online shopping by individuals, businesses, organizations, or enterprises. As much as it is a convenient way of getting services, it can come with a lot of danger. Simply because all these services can be acquired online, and that is an excellent harbor of cybercriminals who are waiting to lay a trap on your system. To be on a safe side, you may need to have the basic knowledge of cybersecurity fundamentals.

What Is Cybersecurity?

It is the process of protecting programs, computer systems,

networks, sensitive information, and software applications. It involves using several techniques, practices, and procedures against cyber-attacks, damage, or unauthorized access.

Cybersecurity is a vital aspect in any organization as it guarantees them the safety of their data. However, in some cases, it tricky solving the cyber-attack menace due to inadequate systems, advanced threats, and attackers. Though, it does not mean it is entirely impossible to get the system going and protect your information at any cost. Let's have a look at some of these attacks and threats affecting information:

Botnets Attacks

Initially, botnets referred to as a network or group of devices connected on the same network to work together. However, this worked in the wrong way. Hackers and other cybercriminals have taken the objective of turning its primary function to create chaos. They do this by injecting malware or other malicious codes to disrupt its normal functioning. It happens due to stealing sensitive and confidential data or emails and also spreading spam emails. In most cases, these attacks are prone to large scale organizations that have a large volume of data at their disposal. These hackers take advantage and manipulate the system to their advantage and creating chaos within the organization.

Crypto-currency Hijacking

In recent times, there has been the use of digital currency and mining. It is so prevalent in the business world, and so is with cybercriminals. They are inventing new ways of using the crypto-currency mining for their convenience on a disruptive and harmful way. They use crypto hacking, a program that injected into the mining systems. It then silently accesses the CPU, GPU, and power resources of the affected system to mine for the crypto-currency inform of Monero coins. It is an advanced threat that gets the hacker using your resources such as the internet and electricity. The process in itself is complex and wears off your system comfortably and later affects its functionality. In most cases, the cryptocurrency traders and their investors are at significant risk.

Ransomware

It is a type of software encryption program file that uses a unique, robust encryption algorithm to encrypt data on a target system. This threat makes it hard to view any files on any application. The authors of this threat have a unique decryption key for the affected systems, which clears them using a remote server. In this case, the hackers involved in its creation will demand a ransom from the affected person to decrypt their data and save their systems. However, this does not guarantee you will have all your data back after paying the ransom.

Phishing

Here a typical kind of attack that involves sending spam emails to people or organizations by imitating legitimate sources. Most of the emails sent through this fraudulent way tend to have secure attachments to confuse you into thinking they came from a real person. For instance, they have active job offers, invoices, offers, and promotions from reputable companies or organizations or can be an email from a higher official of the organization and a government official.

However, the main objective of these emails is to steal sensitive and valuable data such as bank account details, credit card numbers, login credentials, company financial audits, and much more. To rule them out, you need knowledge in phishing email campaigns and their solutions. You can also consider using email filtering options to block the attacks.

Social Engineering Attacks

It is a new attack used by cyber attackers to gather all the sensitive information about an individual or an organization. It comes in the form of displays of attractive prizes, huge offers, and promotions, advertisements. You will fall prey immediately. You provide your bank account details. All the details you provide ere will be cloned and used for fraudulent financial transactions, identity frauds, crimes, and so on.

Since 2007, the ZEUS virus acted as a social engineering attack used for stealing bank account details and other banking related details from unsuspecting people across the world. They not only come with financial issues but can also lead to downloads of highly destructive threats to your system, which may affect its functioning and capabilities.

The History of
Cybersecurity

Cybersecurity is not that old in the technology sector as it dated back to 40 years ago when words like worms, spyware, malware, or viruses meant a different thing. Not only in the information technology sector but for any common man in the business sector, organization, and so on. Since its beginning, it brought mixed reactions as it came as a result of a research project. It is a fantastic fact from the 1970s. Robert Thomas was a researcher for BBN technologies in Cambridge, Massachusetts, at the time he created the computer worm referred to as 'the creeper.' During that time, the creeper infected several computers by attacking one machine after the other with the message; "I'm THE CREEPER: CATCH ME IF YOU CAN."

It was an aggressive threat. Afterward, Ray Tomlinson, the inventor, and creator of email created a similar program referred to as 'the Reaper.' It was to be an antivirus that would delete and clear the creeper.

In the late 1980s, there was another creation of a man called Robert Morris, whose idea was to test the size of the internet. He then wrote a program that would invade the networks, UNIX terminals, and copied itself. The plan referred to was the Morris worm. It was such an aggressive worm that it was disabled and slowed down the functionality of the computer, leaving them unusable. He was the first person to be convicted under the computer fraud and abuse act.

Since then, there has been the creation of invasive, aggressive, and deadliest computer viruses that are prone to cure and are hard to control and detect. That is the main reason that brought about the idea of cybersecurity to help protect data against these deadly attacks.

The Importance of Cybersecurity

Cybersecurity is so critical in an organization or the workplace as the results that felt with its absence are unfriendly. Recently, the increase in threats that led to a lot of damage to individuals and organizations. Handling this cyber menace is hard and needs a lot of effort to ensure all your data is safe and protected from unauthorized persons. There is a need to ensure you have the right strategies to protect your data from threats and minimizing the damages in the event of attacks. However, to be safer, you need a good grip on the knowledge of cybersecurity fundamentals.

Here are the reasons as to why cybersecurity needs implementation at large:

- There is an aggressive rise in threats and cyber-attacks. For this reason, most organizations are finding it necessary to upgrade their cybersecurity not to fall prey to these attacks. It is a common issue and is taking a toll on individual, organization, banking, business information, which later leads to losses and destruction. It has been witnessed in several countries and giving it the attention it requires will save you a lot.

There have been cases where cybercrimes and attacks have cost people up to billions in shillings every year, and that is very alarming.

- There is an increase in techniques and strategies used by the cyber attackers on reaching their targeted persons. They are using more advanced ways to attack, and that has been proven more destructive. They have learned about modern technology and how well to create their malicious threats to affect data to gain profit. That is why you need to learn about cybersecurity and its implementation to keep up with the advancements. It is not that easy mastering all the protective measures, but learning how well to protect your data from the attackers could keep you safe for longer.

- There are new regulations on data protection from GDR, who are expecting every organization to protect the data at their disposal. It is essential due to the increased threats to see to it that your sensitive data is protected and taken care of. In recent times, due to many cases of threats, there are new developments in the courts regarding data theft. To be on the safe side, protecting your information is more important than a long time wasted in the courts.

- Cyber-attacks are very demanding. Once you are affected by threats or attacks, it will take a toll on your resources and organization. There are cases you need to pay ransoms to clear the risks but without surety of getting your information intact. Depending on who took your data, you may end up in reputation breaches and a total financial problem on your business and so on. You can prevent all these scenarios by getting the right preventive measure and ensure your data is protected.

What Are Cybersecurity Fundamentals?

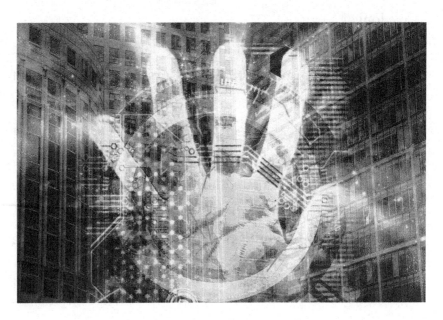

For cybersecurity to be thoroughly analyzed, it follows three basic concepts referred to as 'the CIA Triad,' including confidentiality, integrity, and availability. This model was designed to offer guidance to organizations, institutions, or companies to form an effective security policy. They are essential as their working together will ensure you get the best results in resolving your Cybersecurity issues about information security. These include:

• Confidentiality

This concept is beneficial in limiting the access o any information. It works ion restricting sensitive and vulnerable information from being accessed by third parties such as hackers and cyber attackers. In any organization, for example, there is a need to protect one's information for easy access as that may cause problems if breached. For this reason, organizations and institutions avoid sharing information and educate their workers or colleagues on the effects and how well to protect the data they hold using secure and robust passwords.

You can easily protect your data by handling it differently. You do not have to make the task too complicated. Making the people in an organization have the idea of how dangerous it is to have your information out there for people to access can significantly help. However, at some point, it may prove a daunting task at first but may greatly be improved by sharing experiences with the affected persons.

To ensure there is confidentiality, you can use data classification, data encryption, biometric verification, and two-factor classification as well as security tokens.

- ## **Integrity**

Integrity gives you the guarantee of accurate, trustworthy, correct, and consistent data that is unchanged over some time. To protect your data in the transit from third users, ensure it is original, meaning; the data is not changed, altered, deleted, or allowed illegal access. The safety of data starts with you. Letting other people into your information is very risky.

Putting up proper data protection and security measures in your workplace, institution, or organization will guarantee your data of safety. For this to work, there needs to be user access rules and control as well as file permissions to avoid data breaches and sharing. Ensure a trusted system or person handle the data files. Not everybody can process your information the same way; some may have a hidden agenda.

It is a need to monitor your data against theft, threats, and breaches. All this requires an advanced tool and equipment. These tools ensure your information is intact at all times, and if any risk is detected, the organization will know about it and create ways of amending the issue. In most cases, organizations prefer the use of tools such as cryptographic checksum and checksum to verify their data and information integrity.

Moreover, some attacks or threats can lead to data loss or destruction. For this, there is a need for an effective and reliable backup plan. In most cases, cloud backups are the number one trusted solutions as per now.

- ## Availability

In this case, you need to have your systems in the right condition. Which includes the software, hardware, devices, networks, and security equipment. To give the best results, they should be up to date and well maintained. It will ensure you have proper functionality and easy access to all the data you need without any hindrances. It will also guarantee healthy communication within the system, having a reliable bandwidth.

You will also need to look for types of equipment that are

effective for disaster management. In cases of disaster, system attacks, or threats, there needs to be tools and utilities that will help you solve your issues. In this case, disaster recovery plans, firewalls, effective backup plans, and proxy servers are among the best services you can consider as attack solutions.

For these utilities to work accordingly, they should undergo multiple layers of security to determine the safety of constituents of cybersecurity. In most cases, this feature involves networks, computers, hardware systems, or software programs involving the data shared through them.

For an organization to reap results of safe and reliable data storage and protection, there ought to support from both ends. For instance, in an organization, a practical cyber approach, there is a need to involve the people, computers, networks, processes as well as the technology in large or small scale or individually. Realizing a future with fewer cyber-attacks and threats requires a better organization and support systems that work together. You may also be amazed by how many solutions you can come up with to detect the threats and solve them.

Chapter 5:
What Are the Concepts
of Networking?

Networking is a series of interconnection of computers worldwide to form an overall structure or system. The base or core for networking includes: types of computer networks, types of network equipment/the hardware, Ethernet, wireless local area network, internet service provider, TCP/IP, and other internet protocols and Net routing, switching and bridging.

There are three critical types of computer networks that are geographically based. These include the Local Area Network (LAN), the Wider Area Network (WAN), and the Metropolitan Area Network (MAN). LAN involves the interconnection of computers within a specific locality covering a small geographical area. It is majorly within buildings. There are further three types of LAN technology, which include Ethernet, Token Ring, and Fiber Distributed Data Interconnect (FDDI). The three categories of LAN are based on a specific arrangement of elements in the computer network. Ethernet LANs is based on a bus topology and broadcast communication. The Token Ring LANs are based on a ring topology. The (FDDI) uses optical fibers and an improved Token Ring mechanism based on two rings flowing in opposite directions. The WANs is an interconnection of computers covering a larger geographical area than the LANs, probably between cities and countries. Here, data is transmitted using such media as fiber optic cable and satellite in most cases. It is based on packet switching technology in which information is transmitted over a digital network is grouped into packets. Examples of WAN technology include Asynchronous Transfer Mode (ATM) and Integrated Services Digital Network (ISDN). Metropolitan Area Network is the interconnection of computers covering a much larger geographical area than WANs. The interconnection here is majorly between continents. The equipment sending data in this case to any significant distance is probably sending it to a minicomputer or a mainframe computer. Data is transmitted using terminal emulation software on the personal computer. This is because more extensive networks are designed to be accessed by terminals. A personal computer emulates or imitates a terminal.

Without networks, we wouldn't accomplish much. Just as human networks make us more efficient, so do computer networks. In business, networks are extremely important. All business operations depend on various forms of networking. Networking helps organizations to save time and money. It also helps organizations and individuals to create new streams of income.

Some concepts shape networking. At first glance, these concepts may seem complex. But if you familiarize yourself with the principles of computer networking, it gets easier.

 The reality is that networks are everywhere, and we all work within them. You are used to them to such an extent that you don't even realize it. In this article, we will focus on the concepts of networking. Our main objective is to help you have a better grasp of networking.

A network is a group of several entities that are connected in one way or another. This could be objects or people. It allows the flow of information among the entities involved. However, this has to happen under a set of clear guidelines.

In this piece, we'll be focusing on computer networking. An individual computer can help you accomplish a particular basic task. It undoubtedly boosts your productivity. But when you are using numerous computers that are connected, your productivity becomes greater.

Computers use data networks to process and share important information. Ten staff members can access important information at the same time without sharing a computer. Networking makes it possible for them to do so on different computers. This is made possible by a bunch of interconnected computers. It certainly enhances and promotes coordination within a team working for a common goal.

Imagine what would happen without a network. A team would solely have to rely on one computer to get work done. This could greatly undermine the team's productivity. The team would need a lot of time to complete simple tasks.

Therefore, a computer network can best be described as a group of computers that are linked together. The linking may be done through physical lines. The ultimate goal is to enable efficient exchanging of information in terms of speed and convenience.

When one computer is connected to another, the output is increased. And when several networks are linked together, they form one powerful network. This helps employees to have access to a larger pool of information. With such resources at their disposal, you can rest assured that they can accomplish a lot more.

Components of Network

There are four essential components of a computer network. These are networking devices, end devices, protocols, and the media.

- **End Devices**

Networking takes between devices. End devices play the role of data transmission. They either send or receive various types of data. These are laptops, PCs, phones, or tablets. A network needs at least two devices to function. There are server devices that are tasked with providing data and client devices that depend on the data provided.

- **Media**

Devices have to be connected through a special medium. This

medium is known as the media. There are two forms of media. That's the wired and wireless media.

Wireless media uses signals while wired media uses cables.

- **Protocols**

Protocols are important rules in networking. They aid communication between the devices and also set the standards of communication. Normally, protocols can initiate as well as terminate any form of communication between devices. Also, they encrypt the data before it is sent. The data packaged in a form that can be transmitted within the relevant channels.

- **Networking Devices**

In between devices, there is a networking device. A networking device's main role is to control the flow data between the end devices. It also forwards the data. This device is categorized into three categories. That's the connecting device, securing device, and forwarding device.

Classification Based on Access Type

The classification based on access types includes Intranet,

Extranet, and the Internet.

- **Intranet**

An intranet is a private network. External users can't access this network whatsoever. Not unless they use some unscrupulous methods to do so.

- **Extranet**

An extranet is also a private network. The resources within this network are not available to the public. External are only granted access through a strict authorization process. Full access is not granted to external users. Whatever access they may be given is partial.

- **Internet**

The internet is an open network that anyone with a computer can access. It has a vast resource that the public can utilize.

Classification Based on Relationships between Relevant Devices

This classification is based on the relationship between the end devices. The network is classified into two. That's the peer to peer network and client-server network that will be covered in great detail later.

Networking Plan

When creating a network of computers, you ought to have a network plan. This is because numerous computers are used, hence the need to manage them. Also, you want to ensure that information is kept within particular confines.

The connections should be planned to control the flow of information. Employees should have access to the information that's relevant to their duties. A computer network doesn't mean that everybody in the organization is allowed to access all the information available.

The plan should give clear guidelines on where various types of information should be stored. A plan also defines what information will be accessed by the employees at a given time.

Networking Types and Structures

Networking types are structured differently. They can either be wired or wireless. Also, they could be a combination of both. About a decade ago, most networks were wired. The computer network landscape has since changed. Modern networks mix both wired and wireless connections. Wired networks use Ethernet technology.

Advantages of Wired Networks

- Wired networks are not only reliable but also fast and secure.
- Ethernet ports can also be found in most computing devices, including laptops and desktops.

Disadvantages of Wired Networks

- Wired networks must use cables. And it is costly to run cables.
- Using a wired network within buildings is challenging. This is due to the sophisticated infrastructure. Multiple cables would be required to run between the buildings.
- A wired network doesn't support devices such as smartphones and tablets.

Wireless Networks

Wireless networks don't rely on cables. These networks used the Wi-Fi protocol to transmit data.

Advantages of Wireless Networks

- They are easy to set up. Moreover, you don't require multiple cables running from one point to the other.

- A wireless network offers great flexibility and convenience. They can be used in public places, offices, and homes. Mobile devices use a wireless network. Therefore, you can use all your internet supported devices at your convenience.

Disadvantages of Wireless Networks

- A wireless network is certainly not as secure as a wired network.
- A wireless network is also commonly limited by range. Once you get out of the stipulated range, you can't use it.
- Wireless networks are much slower. The connectivity isn't as fast as it is with a wired network.

Networking Layout and Topologies

To expand a network, the nodes have to be connected. You might not need this in your small office, but as you expand, you'll certainly need it. Though there are many ways to connect these nodes, some of the most common methods include Bluetooth, Wi-Fi, and so on.

These methods of connection are built on various topologies. The common ones are:

- Ring

- Bus
- Mesh
- Hybrid
- Star

Each topology has its strengths and weak points. Wi-Fi and modern Ethernet use a hybrid topology. The hybrid topology is a combination of bus and star. Bluetooth and Wi-Fi can also run on a mesh topology.

Networking Topology – Logical Vs. Physical

The physical connection of network nodes doesn't necessarily dictate how they communicate. Typically, small offices and home networks use the physical bus topology.

- **Peer to Peer Networking**

In peer to peer networking, all the involved nodes are considered to be equal. All nodes can communicate free with each other.

There are no superior nodes with special responsibilities in this kind of networking.

- **Advantages of Peer to Peer Networking**
  - ♦ The peer to peer network doesn't depend on a single node. It is, therefore, unlikely that the failure of a single node will undermine the entire network.
  - ♦ Additionally, peer to peer network isn't sophisticated. This makes it easy to set up.
  - ♦ A peer to peer network is quite reliable and resilient. It doesn't breakdown without a good reason.
  - ♦ This network comes with an excellent distribution of data traffic. And that makes it tremendously effective.
  - ♦ The hardware used in peer to peer networking is inexpensive. So, the initial cost of running this network is affordable.
  - ♦ Most networks require a strong central administrator. However, the peer to peer network doesn't rely on a central administrator.

- **Disadvantages**
  - ♦ It is challenging to secure a peer to peer network. This makes it susceptible to threats.
  - ♦ Every network requires a backup. Nonetheless, peer to peer the network is difficult to back up.

- Locating information on a peer to peer network isn't easy.

- **Client-Server**

A client-server network is based on a superior server. The server is tasked with a special role. For example, it could be a control or a web server.

The client has to connect to the server to use certain services. An example of this type of networking is the internet web.

- **Advantages**

  - The client-server network is administered with the utmost ease.
  - It has a specially dedicated node that makes locating of information extremely easy.
  - A client-server has exceptional safety levels.
  - This network is easy to manage.

- **Disadvantages**
  - Servers can fail. When they fail, the network is jeopardized. These are single points of failure that greatly undermine the entire network.

- The client-server hardware doesn't come cheap. It requires a significant investment, which can be out of rich for both homes and small office owners.
- This network can get concentrated at some point. This may cause some downtime within a network.
- The best modern examples of a client-server network include Twitter, Facebook, and Google Search.

Classification of Computer Networks

Computer networks are classified into various categories. The classifications are based on geographical locations, the relationship between the devices used, and access types.

Classification Based on Geographical locations

LAN-Local Area Network: It links devices within one office or several offices. Ethernet and Token Ring fall within this category.

MAN-Metropolitan Area Network: It is a slightly larger

network with the capacity to connect devices across buildings.

WAN-Wide Area Network: This is a massive network that links devices to multiple devices across countries. A good example of the WAN network includes the Asynchronous Transfer Mode and the Integrated Services Digital Network.

PAN-Personal Area Network: This network is used within a personal area to link devices. It is the kind of network that you use to link your laptop to a printer.

Networking Layers and Protocols

A protocol is a predetermined set of guidelines that dictates how computers should communicate with each other. HTTP is one of the popular protocols, which you may have across in your interactions with computers. This protocol supports communication between a particular web browser and its server.

Good examples of data link protocols include are Wi-Fi and Ethernet. These protocols shape the data as it appears on the media. Both of them use a physical address that's referred to as the MAC address. It has a capacity of 48 bits.

Other popular MAC addresses include the EUI 64 that has 64

bits.

Networking can be divided into numerous layers or levels.

There is the OSI network that utilizes a seven-layer model. Also, there is a common TCP/IP network, which uses a four-layer model. Here are the four levels of the TCP/IP network, and their respective examples:

- Data link-level- Ethernet or Wi-Fi.
- Transport level- UDP or TCP.
- Networking-IP
- Application level-HTTP

As the sending process is progress, these layers add a distinct header to the data. The headers are then systematically eliminated as the data moves towards its destination.

Transmission Control Protocol

TCP provides a safe mode of transmitting data. The transmission takes place through IP packets. The packets have accurate error detection capability. All the data that's transmitted in packets reach as their destination as sent. Data can't be accidentally altered in any way. You can rest assured that the data reaches its destination in its original order.

Before the process of transmitting data is initiated, there has to be a safe connection between the computers involved.

- It is the role of TCP to convert the data into packets.
- Other Applications Protocol in Networking
- FTP (File Transfer Protocol)
- File transfer protocol aids the transfer of various files of data between two computers. The computers need to have an active internet connection.
- Telnet (Terminal Protocol)
- Sometimes, the user needs to connect to a terminal mode. The terminal protocol enables the user to do so.
- SMTP (Simple Mail Transfer Protocol)
- SMTP is a protocol that simply the electronic mail service.

Chapter 6:

Information Tech Guide

Computer technology is used to assist and link people in the contemporary world in many ways. The laptops, desktops, and mobile phones they all network together to perform multiple operations at the same time. The government, individual, and organization depend on these devices for essential things like in the entertainment, food production, communication, education, care, and transportation.

Understanding Information Technology

Information technology – It is the use of a computer, network, storage, and other devices into to secure process, create, store electronic data or information, and exchange all manner of electronic data. Computer technology is the study of computer networks and developing several software programs. It comprises of computer database design, programming, and networking. All these programs correlate to ensure that a computer works properly.

A computer machine is a programmable device that is designed to operate arithmetic and logical operation given by the user and provides a desirable processed output. The computer has two major categories, which are hardware and software. The hardware consists of all layers of physical and tangible components of a computer, such as CPU (central processing unit), keyboard, monitor mouse, and motherboard. While Software is the instructions stored in a computer to run the hardware, these instructions command the computer to perform a specific task, and such Software is operating systems and applications.

Computer technology is any machine that takes commands and calculates the instructions accordingly; the operation can be record-keeping, bailing, planning, and transactions. All these operations take place in a commercially available machine that has been customized according to their functionality. Such machines that are common to our daily process are gas station pumps, ATM, barcode scanners, and

GPS units. However, each of those machines they all rely on circuit boards and digital data to meet the demand and needs of the customer.

Most customers gain improvement in access to services through the internet by ordering products, send emails, scan the barcode through a smartphone, and read reviews before purchasing anything on the website. Most of the programs in television use audio, visual, and animation and special effects in the production of their programs. Audiovisual games employ graphics created by a computer and plugged in a laptop or home-based entertainment where the player can play by themselves or with others using the internet.

The use of applications on the mobile phone can be beneficial in the following ways:

make order in a restaurant, preservation in a hotel, book an appointment with a doctor, purchase movie tickets usually save time that could have been used to wait in a queue.

Hardware

Computer hardware are physical, tangible components of a computer they include. Examples are:

Monitor, control unit (CU), keyboard, mouse, motherboard, central processing unit (CPU), hard driver, random access memory (RAM), and power supply.

1. CPU

It is considered to be the mind of the computer machine that performs all kinds of operations like data processing, storage of data, and instructions. CPU controls all the activities that make up a computer. There are three components of a CPU:

- **ALU (Arithmetic Logic Unit)**

It is the logical part of the CPU in a computer. When you need to carry out mathematical or logical decisions in a computer, the information is carried out by ALU. The ALU contemplates the information in bits. Bits are binary logic 0's and 1" s. They are made up of memories built in the CPU know as registers, which are used to hold data, and data at this point is classified as binary information. They are processed accordingly to instructions.

- **CU (Control Unit)**

It is a component of a CPU in a computer that guides the operation of the processor. It communicates to the computer memory, output, and input devices and ALU on how to respond to the database instruction and does not process any data.

- **Memory**

Memory is a part of a computer that stores data and information that is necessary for functioning. There are two types of memories:

105

o **Ram** – Random Access Memory is the internal memory of the CPU that is responsible for storing data, programs, and the result of an application. The mind is read and writes hence volatile meaning stores data when the computer is working. When the machine is switched off, data is lost or erased. Examples of RAM are Dynamic Random Access Memory (DRAM) - it is a physical memory used in personal computers. This type of memory must be continuously refreshed, or it loses its contents, and it is economical. Static Random Access Memory (SRAM) – this memory is faster and less volatile than DRAM; hence requires more power and very expensive and does not require to be refreshed. Synchronous Dynamic Random Access Memory this memory has a higher processing speed.

o **Read-Only Memory (ROM)** – this type of memory where you can only read, but you cannot write. This kind of memory is non-volatile. The information stored in this memory in permanent, the memory stores instructions that are required to start a computer machine or bootstrap. They are many types of ROM. Examples are MROM (Masked ROM), Programmable Read-only

106

Memory, Erasable and Programmable Read-Only
Memory and EPROM

2. Peripherals

These are devices connected to the computer externally when
these devices are disconnected to the computer will still
function, but the functions performed by the peripheral will
not be available. Examples of peripheral are;

- **Monitor**

A monitor is a visual display unit and is the primary output
device of a computer. They display images as small dots called
pixels that are arranged in a computer in a rectangular form
that sharpens the images. The size of an image will depend on
the number of pixels used.

- **Keyboard**

It is an input device that helps to input data into a computer.
It consists of keys that are responsible for inputting alphabets,
numbers, and special characters into a computer. They can
also navigate using the keyboard to perform a particular
shortcut in a computer machine.

- **Mouse**

It is a pointing device that uses cursor. A control device that has a small box with a corpulent ball at its base, which intellects the movement of the mouse and sends the signals to the CPU to process data.

- **Printer**

It is an output device that is used to print processes data into a paper. Examples of printers are: Impact printers- They write the data by striking the ribbon, which is usually pressed on the document to print. Non-impact printers – this kind of printers print the characters without using the ribbon. They print the whole page of a paper at a time. They are a laser printer, page printer, or inkjet printers.

- **Joy Stick**

This kind of peripherals moves the cursor into a position in a monitor and used in a Computer-Aided Design (CAD).

- **Scanner**

This device allows the user to san printed papers and converts them into a file that is used in a computer device.

Wireless and LTE

These are devices that change electrical signals into waves; they connect a wired network using Wi-Fi. They are three main types of wireless devices which are WAN, PAN, and LAN. Wireless Wide Area Network made through the use of mobile phone signals. They are created and maintained by a mobile phone service provider. Wireless local area network uses radio waves, but the backbone of these networks are sustained using cables with a wireless access point connecting the network. This kind of wireless can be used in a room to being used in an entire university or a hospital. Wireless Personal Area Network (WPAN) they are a form of network that is short in range. They use Bluetooth technology and commonly interconnect compatible devices near the central location. The range of WPAN has a variety of thirty feet.

The devices that are used by networks vary from computers, tablets, phones, and laptops and refer to as clients. When accessing the network through hotspot or use of a router in office or home, the device is referred to as the client. Some router can operate as a client; this can happen when a card is in a computer and connect to other access points or connect to more detached Apps. The Apps can be a standalone device that bridges between a wireless and an Ethernet or a router. The Apps can cover a wide range of areas using wireless networks depending on the power of the computer and type of antenna used by the device.

Some phones, laptops, or wireless router, can support a mode known as Ad-Hoc that allows the device to connect directly together without an access point between that controls the connections. Not all the computers have the Ad-Hoc, and some are hidden. The devices that Ad-Hoc enabled to create a mesh of network, and when they are enabled is called Mesh Nodes.

The wireless network that connects distance areas like two building they need a more focused antenna such as dish antenna. Dish antenna sent thin beams of the network into a specific direction. This long-distance coverage is called point to point connection; this means that two points are connected. The process requires two devices, one configured to the Access point and the other one as a client.

LTE (Long Term Evolution)

It is a term mostly used as 4G LTE and is the standard wireless data. The transmissions that allow one to watch their favorite documentary online or download and watch it later very fast.4g wireless communication was developed by the 3rd generation partnership project that provides ten times the speed of the 3G network on a mobile phone.

The 4G technologies are designed to provide an IP address

based on data, voice, and multimedia streaming.

An Overview of LTE

This is a name given to 3GPP evolved, standard requirement to deal with the increasing data throughout the provision of market. The group that started to work with 3GPPRANstanderdized for LTE in late 2004, and by 20017, all the LTE features that ware related to its functionality ware finished. And in early 2018, most performances specification and protocol ware finished and released.

LTE Requirements

Requirements are written, and defined concept from scuff, absolute fashion, and others meant relation to UTRA nomenclature. The following are LTE design parameters:

- Mobility of up to 350km/h
- Spectrum flexibility, seamless coexistence with other previous technologies hence reduced flexibility and cost
- All systems should support data rates of 100 Mbps in a downlinked 50mbps in the uplink, within a 20MHz bandwidth or a spectral efficiency value of 5bps/Hz and 2.4bps/Hz respectively.

- Downlink and uplink use throughput per MHz at five %point of CDF

The 4g is ten times faster than 3G, can download something at a speed of 22 and 5 Mbps, while 4G is a significant improvement over 3G. Most cellular phones caries and advertise their network as 4G LTE, as it sounds the same as 4G, and some of the cell phones display a 4G LTE. 4G and 4G LTE differences;

The consumer can tell the difference between a 4G and LTE by the speed of downloading something. The mobile phone companies are always updating their cellular LTE network and are closing a gap between a 4G and LTE. The LTE-A is the currently fastest option available right now.

Standard Definitions on Wireless and LTE

Antenna – Converts the electrical signals into radio waves and generally connected to a radio device that transmits the messages into a radio receiver and the interface between the electrical signals in radio and the movement of indicators through the inflight.

Ad-Hoc Network – this is a Device network that is available in a laptop or computer machine connections and is shown as a computer to computer networks. The Ad-hoc can be unplanned or decentralizes network connections.

AP (Access Point) – these are devices that allow other wireless devices to connect into a wired network using Wi-Fi.

Ethernet – This is a type of networking protocol that defines some cable and connections that are used for wiring devices together. In most cases, the Ethernet cabling is categorized into five or six e.g., a cell phone, computer, or tablet.

Node – this is an individual device in a mesh net of the network.

Power over the internet – these describe as the system which passes electrical control along with figures on Ethernet cabling.

Cabling

A cable network is a service delivery that supplies the devices like computer, television or a laptop programs that a user has subscribed to. The availability of such depends on the local franchise area. The number of available channels and networks will depend on some factors. The average cable viewer has the option of viewing more than 150 networks through a cable subscription. The cable system manager decides on the channels and networks to be carried on a specific place. The channel and network are selections are based on the viewer analysis and franchise agreement with the viewer.

Types of Cable Network

They are three different types of a cable network:

Basic, pay and pay per view. The basic network is available per at the lowest and is very popular for people whose budget is limited. There are at least 60 cable channels that can be defined as a first cable network.

The pay cable network is those that charge a flat monthly subscription. The flat-rate payment is required as the network does not run any television advertisement. Hence they need some monthly subscription in order to profit the company. A movie TV station is a good example of such a network.

Pay per view cable network is TV channels that charge a fee for every individual program watched. The pay-per-view program is a network that shows movies that can be rented and viewed. Other programs allow the customer to go and watch the program elsewhere, like the movie theatre.

Choosing a Cable Network

You can only choose one cable network; each cable provider tends to offer cable packages that deliver different Laval of programs. An example, a basic cable network may provide 60 channels, and premium offers over 100 applications. It's only you who can choose the best package that fits your budget.

Advantages of Cabling Network

It is essential to evaluate the cable network before installation. A net that will make use of physical cabling will be more robust and secure compared to wireless network technology.

Security – This is the most important advantage as the cabling network offers a higher level of security than the wireless networks. However, the measure of protection will include the protected WI-FI network and passwords that help to improve the safety of a wireless network. Hence they can never be securing than the cable network.

Speed – not all the cable networks will provide speedy connections, but the newer types of twisted data cabling can operate up to 10 gigabits. An example is a fiber optic cabling transmits light rather than standard data information, making it optimal for high speed and ranges.

Reduced interference – with a proper installation cabling network will help reduce the interference caused by electrical hitch, known as electrical, mechanical obstruction, and radiofrequency. On the other hand, the wireless network is more susceptible to radio frequency interference.

Consistence connections – Compared to the wireless connection, the cabling is more consistence in connection.

When the data is transferred in wireless connections, there is a lapse in network connections caused by electrical interferences.

Expandability – Each router or a hub will provide support of up to 255devices.

Cybersecurity

Cybersecurity is a process or practice that is designed to protect network programs, devices, and data from being attached, authorized access or damaged.

Significance of Cybersecurity

Most of the co-operations and organization collect and stored in a large amount of data in storage devices, a large amount of the data can contain a large amount of sensitive information. Organization and governmental bodies transmit a large amount of raw data across some network and other devices while doing their business. Cybersecurity is dedicated to protecting the information, the programmers, and the system used to store data. The spying on these data are national insecurity and can lead to terrorism.

For an organization to function and coordinate effectively, they need effective cybersecurity. There are a few elements of excellent cybersecurity. They are:

- Great data security
- Application security
- Network security cloud security
- Endpoint security
- Mobile security
- Disaster recovery continuity plan
- And end-user education on security

The organization is advised to promote proactive measures and adapt more approaches to cybersecurity. The NIST (National Institute of Standards and Technology) issued necessary guidelines on the risk and a framework that recommends a shift on continuous monitoring and data focus approach to cabbing cybersecurity.

How to Managing Cyber Security

The NCSA (National Cyber Security Alliance) gives a recommendation on a top-down approach to cybersecurity, which organization management leads and prioritizing the management of cybersecurity. The NCSA advises all the organizations to be ready and prepared for any eventuality. Cyber risk assessment should be put in place in case of any behavior that impacts the functioning of the organization. The organization should have an outline of the damages that an organization would incur in the case of cyber-attack. The cyber risk assessment should consider any regulation that impacts the way the organization collects, stores, and secures data.

Having the best cybersecurity or combining cybersecurity measures and educating the employees on cyber-attacks is the best effort an organization can do to cab the cyber-attack. It may appear like a difficult task but it always to start small and focus on securing the most sensitive information hence going forward to protecting all the data

In conclusion, information technology helps organizations, individual businesses, and governments to increase their efficiency and improvements in effectively processing information. It helps the consumer to buy and sell new relevant technology devices, thus creating a world of business-minded people. Also, technology creates a safe environment by purchasing and installing CCTV cameras. Regardless, there is a continuity of demand for innovative technology solutions leaving room for advancement.

Network Address

Networks come with an IP address. All devices attached to a network have an IP address. You can locate the device using its IP address.

An IP address (Internet Protocol Address) is assigned to every device in a numerical representation. This is for every device that participates in a computing activity. The device has to be, however, dependent on an internet protocol.

The IPv6 and the IPv4 are the two common versions of the Internet Protocol.

IPv4 has been used since the birth of the internet. It is used both in corporate networks as well as the internet. Networking experts predict that it will be replaced by IPv6 in the future. This is attributed to the fact that the IPv6 has a larger capacity. While the IPv4 is just 32 bits, IPv6 is 128 bits. This means that it can effortlessly accommodate a larger number of devices.

Functions of the IP protocol

During the sending of data, the initial data is decomposed into datagrams. Each datagram has a header. The header consists of the port number of the destination and the IP address.

Datagrams are sent to specific getaways. The process is

successive as the getaways are sent from one getaway to the other. This process goes on until the datagrams reach the intended getaways.

Private and Public IP Addresses

You might have heard of private IP addresses. Such addresses are not routable. They can be used in both business and home networks.

On the other hand, public IP addresses are routable. They travel on the internet.

Assigning of IP Addresses

In case you are wondering how IP addresses are assigned, we will tell you how.

For modern networks, IP addresses are assigned automatically. This happens under the DHCP. It doesn't mean that they can't be assigned manually. It is possible, but only on rare occasions.

Domain Names and IP Addresses

People prefer to use names as a form of address. Names are easy to remember. But computers use numbers. If you type a domain name into a web browser, the system translates into an IP address. A DNS server that's found on the internet is tasked with the translation process.

Data Transmission

There is a lot of data transmission that takes place within a network. How does it take place? Data transmission is done through packet switching. The messages are first segmented into segments that are known as packets. The packets are then transmitted from one computer to the next. Upon delivery, data is then extracted from each of these packets. The original message is then reconstructed.

The packets are well-coiffed. They have a data area and a header. Headers consist of two addresses. That's the source and the destination address. Additionally, the header carries sequencing information that helps to reconstruct the original message.

Importance of Networks

A computer machine has been designed for the sole purpose of manipulating data. When computers are linked together, great things are accomplished. The networks are instrumental in the sharing of information and other resources among people. These resources include the internet, file sharing, and applications.

Networks make it easy for colleagues to communicate either

through email or other platforms available on the internet. The same applies to industrial computers because the information has to be shared constantly.

Networking enables businesses to save money. For example, instead of buying a printer for all your employees, you can use networking to link one printer to many computers. This allows all your employees to share a single printer effectively.

Similarities between Different Types of Networks

Although there are various types of networks, there is a similarity between them. For example, networks share servers. These are computers that are endowed with sharable resources within a particular network.

Other Similarities

The server serves clients. Clients are computers that access depends on the information held on the server. They all access the pool of information offered by a network server.

A Connection medium that enhances the connection of several computers within a network

Another similarity is computer peripherals. Printers and files are also used within different networks.

As you can see, computer networking is a well-structured

process that makes work easy. Government agencies and business organizations use to rely on networking to streamline their functions. Networking saves such organizations millions of dollars every year.

Besides that, networking helps organizations to work more efficiently. Teams can tackle various projects with much ease when they network.

Networking aids the sharing of important information between the involved parties. Organizations store massive information. It is difficult to store, manage, and process the data manually. Moreover, organizations are large. And all the data that's gathered and used can be overwhelming.

Apart from the complex duties that simplified by networking, there are other minor but equally important functions. For example, networking aids the configuration of various computers in an office. This enables the employs to share the fax machine, or a printer through a network.

It is not only a large organization that benefits from networking. In this digital area, all types of businesses depend on networks. Therefore, it is important to be familiar with the concepts of networking.

Chapter 7:

What Are the Best Network Monitoring Tools?

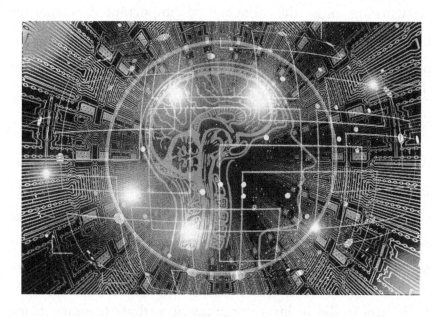

Networking is also referred to as computer networking. It is a term used to refer to transportation and exchange of data between nodes through a universal medium in the information system. Networking involves using a network, designing construction, managing, maintaining, and operating the network software, infrastructure, and policies.

Networking allows for the connection of devices and endpoints together on a local area network or a bigger network. This is one of the most effective services that business owners all over the world can take advantage of. Computer networking provides valid and reliable ways of resources and information sharing within an organization or a business. It helps people to benefit from their information technology equipment and systems.

The significant benefits of networking include:

File sharing – Data can be easily shared among different users. Data can as well be accessed remotely when it is kept on other connected devices.

Resource sharing – Computer networking helps in sharing resources between different peripheral devices connected to the network. They include copiers, scanners, and printers. Resource sharing helps to save money because the software can as well be shared among different users.

Sharing one Internet connection – Having a single internet connection is cost-efficient and enhances the protection of systems when the network is adequately secured.

Increasing the storage capacity – Networking allows for the access of multimedia, and vital files when they are stored remotely in other networks- connected storage devices and machines.

Computer networking also improves communication in that customers, staff, and suppliers easily share information and keep in touch. It allows for everyone interested in business access common databases, thus avoiding duplication of data, preventing errors, and saving time. Networking also makes it easier for organizational staff to work on queries, thus delivering better standards of service. The improvements are possible because of customer's data sharing through the networks.

Computer networking also has incredible benefits on costs. Information is stored in one standard and centralized database, thus increasing the efficiency of the drive and reducing costs. Staffs are able to deal with many customers in little time because they are all accessing product and customer databases. Minimum IT support is also required because network administration can be efficiently centralized. Sharing of internet access, and peripherals sharing cam also help in cutting costs.

Improving consistency and reducing errors are other significant benefits of computer networking. This is because all staff in a business or organization are accessing similar information and from a single source. It allows for the easier making of standard version manuals and directories accessible to each staff. Backing up of data from individual points on a scheduled basis provides for consistency.

The skills required when operating computer networking entirely depends on the network's complexity. Large enterprises, for instance, may have more security requirements due to multiple nodes. Such companies, therefore, require experienced network administrators who can successfully manage and maintain the network. This may be different from smaller organizations whereby there are few nodes involved, thus requiring less security.

Basic Fundamentals of Computer Networking

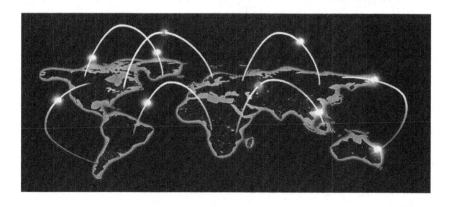

Computer networking has been in existence for quite a long time, and as years go by, advancements continue to be made.

Networking involves multiple devices such as routers, computers, and switches being connected to each other through wireless signals or cables. Building a wireless network needs one to understand all the basics of joining networks.

Many people have an aim of becoming expert IT technicians, and understanding only the hardware may not be so helpful to them. Many people get stuck at the networking point due to misunderstandings. The paragraphs below will explain some of the basic fundamentals of networking. They will give an understanding of how computers communicate through networks. Understanding the interaction and communication between computers is essential to anyone who wants to become a networking administrator.

Networking protocols are essential for developers dealing with applications relating to servers that use JAVA or programming based on Socket, such as bash or python, as well as System Admin. Computer networking is done through diverse sets of IP protocol suites. The most popularly used protocols include IP and TCP. IP is an abbreviation for Internet Protocols. Each of the protocols has unique architecture, as well as diverse functionalities.

The Internet Protocol

The internet protocol gives the definition of the networking communication protocols principals. It is helpful in relaying many datagrams through network boundaries. The internet protocol's primary purpose is providing routing functions that help in the establishment of inter-networking connection, enabling the internet. The primary function is delivering packets from one host to the other host while depending on present IP addresses. The IP addresses are available on the packets' headers.

The internet protocols have four layers, with each layer having a set of instructions it carries out. The four layers include the application layer, the data link layer, the network layer, and the transport layer.

1. The Basic Fundamental of Networking Layer – The Application Layer

The application layer appears at the topmost of IP and TCP protocols in networking. The primary purpose of the layer is transferring data through computers from a particular end to the other. The application layer works in conjunction with processes and applications using transport layer protocols.

The processes and applications transport explicit instructions that help in the execution of tasks and enhances communication with the second layer. Application layer protocols have the following elements.

Hypertext transfer protocol that is commonly applied in modern webs. It provided a base for the founding of the World Wide Web. The protocol acts in the form of requesting and responding. It engages in multiple activities for the client.

File transfer protocol engages in the transfer of data to several networks. Its main tasks involve transferring and controlling data between computers using client and server architecture models. In many cases, the protocol can either use a password for authentication or can anonymously and automatically connect.

A simple mail transfer protocol is used when transmitting emails. The protocol is based on texts. It consists of three elements the MAIL that determines the returning address, RCTP allowing for connection with the recipient, and DATA acting as the message's body.

The simple network management protocol is based on IP addresses. Its principal function is consistently collecting information on IP addresses from different

133

machines. There are many devices that support the use of a simple network management protocol. There are also many diverse versions of the particular protocol.

2. The Basic Fundamental of Networking – The Presentation Layer

The presentation layer works on the translation or converting data, for instance, encoding character, and compressing data between software applications, and networking devices. It is considered to be efficient when dealing with secure transactions such as money transfer and banking. It is useful because it allows for encryption and decryption of such reliable data. The presentation layer also helps in the conversion of formats.

3. The Networking Session Layer

As a basic fundamental in networking, the networking session layer has the responsibility of opening, closing, and managing end-user application's sessions. The sessions can include many requests and responses taking place inside the software. The layer also facilitates the combinations of packets as well as sorting them in an appropriate order.

4. The Transport Layer

The task of the transport layer is communicating with the application layer about transferring data to the necessary hosts. In performing its role, the transport layer uses the transmission control protocol in most cases due to its reliability. The control protocol helps in the transmission of data from the application layer into smaller sizes of data and later transferring them one by one to the network. It is commonly used when people want to download and upload large files. It ensures there is no loss of packets that could lead to the corruption of downloaded and uploaded data.

5. The Networking Network Layer

The networking network layer is also referred to as the internet layer. Its main purpose is to route data above networks. The Internet protocol is used when differentiating addresses. The internet control message protocol is commonly used in commanding the ping to check on whether the host is active. It also sends error messages through the network, describing if a host is not responding or is down.

6. The Networking Data Link Layer

It is also referred to as the Network Interface Layer. Its main function is providing drivers for diverse devices found in the

Operating System. The drivers communicate and transfer data to networks. The network interface card facilitates communication between devices. The transfer of data is done either through cables or wirelessly through routers and Wi-Fi. The significant protocols used in transferring data are the address resolution protocols and point to point protocols.

7. The Networking Physical Layer

The physical networking layer is a vital layer found in the OSI computer networking model. It comprises of networking hardware. It is considered to be the most complex layer in networking due to the diversity of networking devices that are available. Its primary function is transferring raw bits over physical hardware through nodes used for the connection. It comprises of the hardware, including the wireless hardware consisting of Wi-Fi, connectors, cables, and network interface cards.

Understanding Cyber Security

Cybersecurity is also referred to as computer security or information technology security. It is the act of protecting computer systems from damage or theft to their software, hardware, and electronic data. It also means preventing the misdirection and disruption of computer systems from the services they are responsible for providing.

The increase in dependence on computer systems, wireless networks, and the internet has led to the popularity in the field of cybersecurity. It is one of the most concerned matters in the contemporary world due to overgrowing cases of cyber-attacks and threats. Due to its complexity, cybersecurity has also become one of the challenges facing the technology field today.

Cyber attackers are making use of more refined techniques to target and attack computer systems. Small and large organizations, as well as individuals, are being impacted by these cyber threats and attacks. They have considered cybersecurity as a priority in their everyday operations. The focus is on coming up with the best measures to control and eliminate cyber threats and attacks. Employees in organizations are being trained on the best measures to deal with cyber-attacks. Almost everything we do today is linked to the internet, thus increasing chances for vulnerabilities, flaws, and breaches.

Cybersecurity is defined as a process and techniques that are involved in the protection of sensitive data, networks, computer systems, and software applications from potential cyber-attacks. Cyber-attack is a terminology used in covering multiple topics. Most of the common issues covered by cyber-attacks include exploitation of resources, disruption of the normal functioning of businesses and processes involved, tampering systems, and the data stored in them, unauthorized access to sensitive information and targeted systems, and use of ransomware attacks in encryption of data and extortion of money from victims.

Cyber-attacks have been quite innovative, and attackers can disrupt security and hack computer systems. Businesses, therefore, have to come up with strategies through which they can effectively fight back the dangerous attacks. Understanding the importance of cybersecurity needs one to recognize some common forms of attacks and threats.

Ransomware – This is a software program involved in file encryption. It uses exceptional algorithms in robust encryption in encrypting files within the targeted system. Ransomware threat authors, applies a rare key for each target, saving each on a remote server. Users are, therefore, unable to access these files through any application. The attackers take advantage of the situation by extorting money from the victims for decryption of data or providing the decryption code.

Botnets Attacks – The main reason for designing botnets was for them to perform particular tasks in a group. Cyber attackers are, however, using them for all the wrong purposes. They use it by accessing and injecting malware or malicious code that disrupts the functionality of the network. Common botnets include spreading spam emails, stealing of personal data, and distributed denial of service. Large-scale organizations and businesses are primary victims of botnets attacks because of colossal data access.

Social engineering attacks – Cybercriminals are using social engineering attacks strategy to gain computer user's sensitive details. The tactic involves tricking users through attractive prizes, advertisements, huge offers, and requesting the user to feed their confidential and bank account information. The information that users feed is cloned and used in identity and financial fraud.

Cryptocurrency Hijacking – Cryptocurrency hijacking is a new addition in the modern cyber world. Advancement in digital mining and currency has led to an increase of cyber-crimes. Cybercriminals are coming up with ways through which they can benefit from cryptocurrency. Traders and investors who focus on cryptocurrency are becoming primary soft targets for this form of attack. The hijacking process involves designing and injecting mining codes silently to the computer systems. The crypto jacker uses power resources, GPU, and CPU of the target system in mining for cryptocurrency. Monero coins are particularly mined utilizing this kind of technique. The target victim usually incurs the vast internet and electricity bills. The lifespan of the victim devices is also reduced.

Phishing – This is a common cyber-attack whereby the attacker sends a spam email and attempts to imitate any legitimate source. Emails sent through phishing usually have strong messages and are followed by attachments such as big job offers, and an invoice. The aim of the attacker is to steal confidential and sensitive data. They are able to gather information such as credit card numbers, login credentials, and information on bank accounts. Email filtering techniques can help one in avoiding such attacks.

Experiencing cyber-attacks has become so prevalent in most organizations and businesses today. It is vital to research techniques being applied and the measures to avoid these attacks. Educating oneself on the basics of cybersecurity and its use can as well reduce the risks of being attacked.

Cybersecurity is a broad term based on three major concepts. The concepts are named "The CIA Triad." This means that it is comprised of confidentiality, integrity, and availability. The model was designed to act as a guide to businesses and organizations on crucial policies involved in cybersecurity in information technology.

1. Confidentiality

These are the rules that provide some limitations to accessing information. Confidentiality consists in taking appropriate measures to eliminate the risks of confidential and sensitive information being accessed by cyber hackers and attackers. In most organizations and large-scale businesses, people are either denied or allowed access to information depending on how it is categorized. The right person in each department is authorized to access the information. Proper training is also given to these people about using strong passwords to secure their accounts and sharing information. Data protection is enhanced by changing how data is handled.

2. Integrity

Integrity guarantees accuracy, trustworthiness, and consistency of data over a period. It ensures that the data in transit is not altered, deleted, changed, or illegally accessed. Appropriate measures are taken to ensure the safety of the data. A data breach is controlled through user access and file permission control measures. Change or breach in particular data can be detected by the use of appropriate technologies and tools. Regular backups help in coping with potential data loss, unintended deletion, or cyber-attacks.

3. Availability

Availability means that all essential components, such as devices, networks, software, hardware, and security tools, should be adequately maintained and consistently upgraded. This helps in ensuring the proper functioning and data access without disruption. It also means providing consistent communication between multiple components by giving adequate bandwidth. Availability also means providing diverse equipment for security in case of any cyber-attacks. Disaster recovery plans, reasonable backup solutions, firewalls, and proxy servers are efficient utilities in coping with cyber-attacks.

Chapter 8:
Types of Firewall

A firewall is a kind of cybersecurity tool that protects a computer network from being tempered or compromised: preventing attacks from hackers who try breaking into the system from outside. Firewalls can be in various forms; it can be in the form of a software or hardware on a computer. For a firewall to work efficiently, it has to be connected to at least two network interfaces with one protected and the other that is exposed to attacks or threats. Therefore, you can consider a firewall to a form of gateway installed between two sets of a network.

How Do Firewalls Work?

Having known what firewalls are and what they do, it is time you learned how they work! Firewalls work by examining all the available data packets that pass through them to assess whether they meet the guidelines and regulations posed by the Access Control List (ACL) and created by the person administrating the network. If the data packets meet the rules set by ACL, they will be allowed to maneuver inside the connection.

Additionally, firewalls play a critical role in keeping a log of essential procedures and activities occurring within a network. Again, the necessary actions are only identified by the administrator. He then configures the related firewall to keep the logs basing on the level of importance.

The process of filtering logs can be done basing on several things, including the packet attributes, address, state, and protocols. Firewalls, however, only display the packet headers on screens.

Having known how firewalls work, we next discuss the types of firewalls. Read on to find out!

The Types of Firewalls

Firewalls are categorized into different types. This is done depending on the level of security they provide and the advancement they have. Below, we discuss extensively on the types of firewalls in existence today.

- **The Packet Filtering Firewall**

This is a type of firewall that is usually installed on routers that connect or link the network in the inside to the internet. The package filtering firewall is only implemented on the OSI model of a network layer. It works based on the rules defined by the Access Control Lists. Packet filtering firewalls work by checking the whole set of packets provided and verify them against the set of instructions provided by the administrator through the ACL. In situations where a package doesn't meet the set of rules defined by the administrator, that packet gets dropped immediately, and logs are informed and update accordingly. When using packet filtering firewalls, administrators have the power to build their ACL basing on the protocol, address, and packet attributes.

- ○ **Advantages of Packet Filtering Firewalls**

  - ♦ One of the significant benefits of packet filtering firewalls is that they are very affordable.

146

- ◆ Packet filtering firewalls also need lower resource usage to make them cost-efficient.
- ◆ Additionally, they are the best suited for those of us with smaller networks.

○ **Disadvantages of Packet Filtering Firewalls**

- ◆ As we mentioned earlier, the packet filtering firewalls only work network layers, and they cannot work on complex instruction based type of models.
- ◆ Additionally, packet filtering firewalls are also very vulnerable, especially to spoofing on most occasions.

- • **The Circuit Level Gateway Firewalls**

This is a type of firewall that is installed at session layers of any OSI model. They are used to monitor events and sessions such as the TCP multiple way handshakes to determine whether the connection requested is legit or not. In circuit-level gateway firewalls, the significant and vital screening takes place before the link is launched. The information channeled to a computer device on the other side of the network via circuit-level gateway looks to have come from a portal. This feature plays a vital role in establishing cover stealth for private networks from strangers.

- **Advantages of Circuit Level Gateway Firewalls**

  - Just like the Packet Filtering Firewalls, the circuit-level gateway firewalls are also very affordable and cost-friendly.
  - Circuit Level Gateway Firewalls also give the private network anonymity, making it very secure from threats and hackers.

- **Disadvantages of Circuit Level Gateway Firewalls**

  - One of the significant drawbacks of the circuit-level gateway firewalls is they are not able to filter the individual packets. This makes them very vulnerable because once a connection is established, hackers can take advantage of it.

The Application of This Kind of Firewalls

The gateway firewall circuit levels are applied in many

dimensions of technology in today's world. The application-level gateways, for instance, are used in the layer one in the application of an OSI tool and can give security and protecting the specific Application Layer of the Protocol in question. One good example of the level application Gateway Firewalls is the proxy server. This kind of firewall, however, can only work with protocols that are highlighted. A good example is, if you installed a web application basing on a firewall, it only will be able to enable the HTTP Protocols Data. The Circuit level gateway firewalls are meant to understand app-specific commands like the HTTP: POST and HTTP: GET as installed on application layers for Special Protocols.

Additionally, the application level firewalls can also be used as the caching servers that play an essential role in improving network performance, making it easier to log the level of traffic.

The Stateful Multilayer Firewall

This firewall is made of a combination of all the firewalls we have discussed so far. They are very advanced firewalls and complex in equal measure. Stateful Multilayer Inspection Firewalls can be used to filter the packets in network layers through the use of ACLs.

Additionally, the Stateful Multilayer Inspection firewall also checks for the single sessions provided on the session layers as well as evaluating packets on the ALG. This type of firewall is compatible with transparent mode enabling direct linkage and connections between the server and the client, something that wasn't possible a few years ago. The Stateful multilayer inspection firewall implements the algorithms and critical security models that are specified by protocols; hence, in the long run, making data transfer and connections easier and secure.

The Proxy Firewalls

These kinds of firewalls operate in application layers with the primary purpose of filtering the incoming traffic between the current network and the source of traffic; this explains the name 'proxy firewall.' Proxy firewalls are transported through a cloud-based tool or a different proxy element. Instead of allowing traffic link up and connect directly, it first identifies a relationship or connection to the origin of traffic and verifies the data packets that come in.

This kind of inspection can be compared to that of a Stateful multilayer inspection firewall because it focuses on both the TCP multiple way handshake protocols and the data packets. Proxy firewalls, however, can also carry out deep-layer packet checks and inspections, verifying the real contents of the information-carrying package to ascertain it has no malware.

Upon completion of the check and the data, the packet is given the green light to proceed to the destination; the proxy firewall transfers it off. This procedure builds another layer of gap or separation between the individual devices on operating on your network and the client. This enables them to make another layer of anonymity hence securing your network.

The major advantage of Proxy Firewalls is that they are more secure thanks to the extra layer of anonymity created. They are also pocket-friendly and affordable.

If there is any setback when using proxy firewalls, is that they can slow down the entire internet because they require more steps during the data packet transfer process.

The Software Firewalls

This refers to any firewalls installed on a local device instead of a separate piece of hardware. One of the significant advantages of software firewalls is that they are critical when defensive measures by separating the individual network point end from each other.

One of the significant setbacks of software firewalls, however, is that maintaining them on different sets of devices can be time-consuming and extremely difficult. Additionally, some tools on the network connection may not be compatible with any of the software firewalls. In such occurrences, you will, therefore, have to use various software firewalls for every asset.

Hardware Firewall

This is one of the most popular types of firewalls in the world. The hardware firewall is applied majorly in the modern-day networks as either a LAN network or a border device (used to protect internally placed LAN networks acquired from the internet or any other unwarranted networks) or protecting the internal systems in more significant enterprises. The hardware firewalls mostly have a lot of physical network attributes that can be applied in creating various security zones that are different from Layer 3 elements. Every physical tool can be categorized further into sub-interfaces that, when well propagated, can help expand the secure zones.

When the hardware firewall is operating on its separate hardware application, it can handle vast volumes of data packets as well as millions of network connections. Hardwire firewalls work best in generally high performing machines. The feature that makes the hardware firewall one of the best firewalls to work with is the ability to keep hackers and threats at bay. They are well advanced to alert the administrator of any potential risks and how they can deal with them. Hardware firewalls are, however, more expensive compared to the other firewalls.

Some of the most popular brands that use the hardwire firewall are FortiGate, Checkpoint, Sonic Wall, and Palo Alto.

The Application Firewall

Just as its name goes, the application firewall is a type of firewall that operates at layer seven of the operating system model. Its primary functions are controlling and inspecting the data packets at every application level. This firewall has information about what a typical application should have and that a malicious use contains. It is, therefore, well equipped to filter out any unwarranted access.

For instance, the app firewall that secures a website server has knowledge of the web associated HTTP attacks such as cross-site crippling, and it guarantees the application from such threats by checking into HTTP app traffic. Some of the popular elements that use the application firewall are the Web app firewall. The website app firewall protects the traffic from internet users that come in towards the computer network. Application firewalls are fast gaining popularity thanks to its affordable pricing. It is also one of the most efficient firewalls that help keep threats and hackers at bay.

The Next Generation Firewalls

The next-generation firewall is a term mostly used by manufacturers to refer to a brand of firewalls that are advanced and use high technology standards. What this means is that the next generation firewall combines almost all the firewalls we have discussed above. It is a state of the art kind of firewall that gives application-level inspection and protection.

The next-generation firewall provides comprehensive analysis and inspection and can locate corrupted traffic in all the layers of the OSI model and any layer associated with it. It contains a host of advanced features, including antivirus features, intrusion detection, and prevention, among others.

These features are, however, licensed separately, forcing any interested buyer to spend a little more money to activate all the protections. A good number of next-generation firewalls establish communication using the cloud service security that belongs to the manufacturer to obtain the threat level information from the secure cloud.

What makes next-generation firewalls very efficient is that they have a combination of other features that are well advanced and able to deal with potential threats and incoming hacker detection. The feature that makes the next-generation firewalls one of the best firewalls to work with is the ability to detect security threats even with the slightest detection of malicious activity. They are well advanced to alert the administrator of any system dysfunctions and how they can deal with them. The next-generation firewalls are, however, more expensive compared to the other firewalls. The reason behind this, however, is that they are more advanced and sophisticated compared to any other firewall.

The Stateful Inspection Firewall

A majority of the modern-day firewalls put into use the feature of tasteful inspection. This might be difficult to understand, and the example highlighted below will help you comprehend it.

In a communication medium between a server and a client (for instance, a person with a website browser engaging in a conversation with a web server), the indicated client browser will initiate an HTTP communication with the server serving the website at port 80. Now assuming that this firewall (the state inspection firewall) allows the HTTP traffic being transferred to pass through it, the data packets will, therefore, be able to reach the servers, which will initiate an instant reply as it is the case with every TCP communication model.

The stateful inspection firewall will store the initiating link that exists between the client, and the server is what is called a state table. The table will have information about details such as the destination IP, the source IP, TCP flags, and the destination ports. This means that any reply coming in from the external web servers that are similar to the connection installed before will have to go through the firewall first then reach the designated servers without the need for extra configuration. The above-mentioned process makes setup easier since the user doesn't have to apply any set of rules on the firewall to reply to the incoming data packets. The data packets mentioned above will instead be allowed automatically only if they are associated with the already installed network connection from the client to the server.

The feature that makes the stateful inspection firewalls one of the best firewalls to work with is the ability to detect security threats even with the slightest detection of malicious activity. They are well advanced to alert the administrator of any system dysfunctions and how they can deal with them. The stateful inspection firewalls are, however, more expensive compared to the other firewalls. The reason behind, however, is that they are more advanced and sophisticated compared to most of the firewalls.

Telephony-Related Firewalls

Just as its name goes, the telephony related firewalls are a type of firewall that operates at layer seven of the operating system model. The primary functions of telephony related firewalls are controlling and inspecting the data packets at every application level. This firewall has information about what a regular application should have and that a malicious use contains. It is, therefore, well equipped to filter out any unwarranted access.

For instance, the app firewall that secures a website server has knowledge of the web associated HTTP attacks such as cross-site crippling, and it ensures the application from such threats by checking into HTTP app traffic. Some of the popular elements that use the application firewall are the Web app firewall.

The website app firewall protects the traffic from internet users that come in towards the computer network. Application firewalls are fast gaining popularity thanks to its affordable pricing. It is also one of the most efficient firewalls that help keep threats and hackers at bay.

Chapter 9:

Understanding

Cybersecurity

Cybersecurity is the protection of computers' mobile devices, servers, networks, data, and electronic systems from cyber-attacks and malicious viruses. Cybersecurity an also refer to as information technology security. Cyber securities are designed to protect and maintain the confidentiality of the data stored in the internet-connected systems. The organization should have a secure and effective respond to cyber-attacks. The purpose of installing such security measures is to prevent data breaches and identity theft. Cybersecurity is classified into the following categories:

- **Information security**

The protection of data from unauthorized personnel. Goals of securing data protect the confidentiality of the data and preserve the integrity of information either in storage or in transit.

- **Application security**

The procedure of developing, adding, and testing safety features in an application to prevent security attacks against opportunistic malware. A conceded application could make available access to information designed to protect the device. Adequate security always begins at the designing of the app even before the application is installed.

- **Network security**

They are policies and practices implemented to break and monitor accessibility, modification, and misuse of computer or mobile network from unauthorized. The security of the network mostly involves authorizing access of information to authorized persons and usually controlled by the administrator. Network users are assigned by passwords and authority information to access data and programs that are within their security clearance.

- **Operational security**

Operational security includes the processes that recognize and identifies critical information, also determine whether the information, if accessed by malicious individuals, could be useful to them. Operational security also executes and selects a measure that removes any exploitation of helpful information.

- **Disaster recovery and continuity of business**

It is a planning strategy that is capable of restoring data and critical information in inventing that the system was hacked or destroyed during the disaster. When protecting your data, it is good to understand and plan. The plan arises when the application and usage of information after disaster tricks. Continuity of business includes a strategy and action that guarantees that the business will continues after the disaster.

- **End-user education**

The cybersecurity starts with your employees. The end-user is the specific person who uses the hardware device or software program after installation in the machine. Make sure that you educate your employees or yourself on the matter concerning software program or device. The end-user education plays a vital role in keeping the information of the organization safe. The end users are the first line of protection against cyber-attacks.

Importance of Cybersecurity

Cybersecurity considers as most important to an organization, government, institution, and individual. It is essential to protect the family and loved ones from cyber fraud and identity theft. Most of the cyber-attacks happen because of lack of awareness. Cybersecurity has always evolved since the discovery of computers. The modern-day the cyber attackers have improved their tactics in breaking down the systems also installed the internet has improved, making it easier to attack the businesses.

The attackers have developed tools that are designed to exploit the weaknesses of the computer or mobile device. Most hackers do not attack the network, but the website or the server of the organization or individual. Hackers find it difficult to hack the network, as the most network of the organization has a firewall installed hence problematic for them to access. The following are the requirement for cybersecurity:

- Firewall
- Web filtering software
- Endpoint protection
- Intrusion prevention systems
- Radius server
- Logging software
- Encryption

Organizations and businesses can suffer a large amount of money when they fail to safeguard and handle confidential data effectively. There are numerous methods to use to make sure that your data is safe.

An example is hardening, which means that confidential data stored in the corner of a structure, meaning that the information stored inside of a hard shell that cannot be cracked. Placing logging software, any hacker who attempts to access the information in the hardened network will be logged and traced. Installing and using VPNs and encrypted links makes it harder for hackers to access your data. Most hackers will not invest too much to hack into a new security system. It takes time to hack the system, thus increasing the chances of getting caught.

Honeypot is another method of cybersecurity. Placing the right software in the system, any connection that goes in and out of the network can be traced fast. This area of the network is set deliberately and makes the network seem vulnerable. When the hacker attacks the systems, they go straight to the vulnerable area of the net. When they reach there, they steal files and later find out that the data are empty and leave a trace that they were attacking the system.

When cyber network security is secure, the attackers will use a method of social engineering. Social engineering is the method of sending emails telling them to click here. Social engineering has evolved from being told to click here to taking place in internet browsing. Hackers apply the following tactics, phishing, vishing, smishing, and whaling. It is difficult to access the information that was lost since it appears that the data was gladly given. In social engineering, even the smallest mistake of giving out a password to a user account is enough to provide access to hackers to hack data and confidential information about the organization.

Salami cyber-attack hackers steal little money from several banks that lead to a large amount. These attacks can go undetected since the nature of the type of cybercrime.

An electrical protocol should be put in place to detect malware in real-time. The use of heuristic analysis is to observe the behavior of an application or a program to protect it against viruses that change their shape. The organization should train and educate and make them understand their part in keeping the data of the organization protected and report any malicious activity. The organization should put plans in place to deal with any attacks effectively and respond keenly to reduce the impact of the attack on the business.

Data Security Measures and Its Importance

We live in a world where most people use electronic devices & systems in almost every deal and transaction. Technology has resulted in many computer networks and electronic systems, and indeed, they all deal with data. What you might not know is that data one element considered to be very valuable, and internet users are very keen to find out how their information and personal data are handled. Data is, therefore, a precious asset and can have a massive impact on people. It needs severe protective measures to ensure information is secure and brings us to what we shall be discussing in this article: data security and its importance.

What Does Data Security Mean?

Data security refers to the technical process of safeguarding data and keeping it from corrupted and unauthorized access. It isn't all types of data that are essential and sensitive, but others are precious and essential. Having unauthorized people get access to that kind of information can cause a lot of problems because they can use them to do things they are not allowed to do. Data security, therefore, is a defensive measure established to help keep data safe and out of reach for any unauthorized access. There exist a lot of ways you can protect data, as we have discussed below.

The basic concepts of any data security system are confidentiality, integrity, and, lastly, availability. The three concepts are commonly abbreviated as CIA. It is the underlying security model guiding organizations and companies to protect their valuable data from unauthorized people and hackers. Now let's break down each of the concepts and find out what they mean.

- Confidentiality is a concept that makes sure data is available to individuals with authorized access and does not fall in the wrong hands.
- Integrity makes sure that data is accurate and well reliable.
- Availability, on the other hand, is a virtue that makes sure data is readily accessible to serve the needs of clients.

So, what should you consider when setting up data security? Discussed below are some of the essential things you ought to consider when coming up with a security model.

Where is the valuable data placed or located? You can't say you are protecting something if you have no idea where that thing is put.

The other thing you should consider is who can access your sensitive data? If you have no records of people allowed to access sensitive data, leaves you at high risk if getting accessed by an unauthorized individual. Know who has access to your data because it will give you an idea of the kind of person you are dealing with, and it makes it easier for you to pinpoint any unauthorized access.

Have you actualized the consistent checking and instant alerting on the data? Activating real-time alerts and establishing a continuous monitoring process will ensure the security covers all high alert areas. The real-time alerts play a role in detecting any malicious activity, unwarranted access, and alerts the user before it gets too late.

Below we look at the types of data security, let us discuss some of the technologies used in data security.

Data Security Technologies

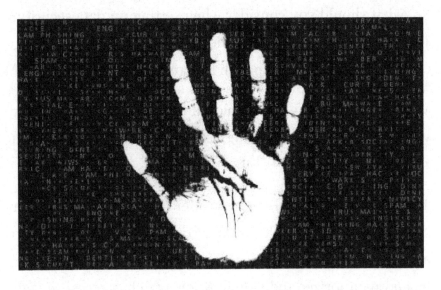

Discussed below are some of the technologies applied in data security today. They are used to reduce the risk involved as well as preventing the security breaches.

- **Data Auditing**

Auditing data when a security breach occurs plays a critical role in preventing it from happening again. Data auditing helps discover essential details of what might have caused the violation. It revealed the people that had access to data during the time of the security breach, how it happened, and the path followed when accessing the file. This kind of technology, therefore, plays a vital role in the process of investigation.

Apart from that, when advanced data auditing solutions are implemented, the information technology administrators can have access to critical visibilities needed to keep unauthorized access at bay.

- **The Real-Time Data Alerts**

In typical situations in today's world, it will take several months for a company to notice they have been breached. One sad fact is that the majority of the companies realize there has been a security breach from their customers or other sources, instead of getting the information their information technology departments.

The real-time data alert technology and constant monitoring of data activity make it easier for you to able to detect security breaches, accidental destruction, as well as unwarranted access to critical personal data.

- **The Data Risk Assessment Technology**

In light of what we have discussed earlier, the data risk assessment technology plays a crucial role in helping organizations know their most vulnerable kind of data and give information about how it can be fixed. The process of doing so starts by identifying the data that is very important and vulnerable, and it can be easily accessible. The risk assessment technology gives a summary of all the found details giving complex feedback on the level of vulnerability and alerts you where you need to work on first.

- **Minimize Data**

During the last ten years of information technology, there has been a significant shift in how people perceive data. In the past, people preferred having more data than less. The more data you had, the more ahead you were.

In today's world, however, data is more of a liability. The potential loss of billions of shillings, securing breach that can destroy the reputation of an entire company as well as the hefty fines associated with collecting more data than what is recommended makes data a very risky asset.

In that connection, it is advised to have only the data you require. Don't ask for people's telephone numbers and home addresses when you only need their identification numbers.

Having learned the data protection technologies, we move on to the types of data protection. Read on to find out!

Types of Data Security

As we have learned earlier, data security protects sensible and vulnerable data from unauthorized access. Almost everything in today's world revolves around computers and the Internet. Music and entertainment transport and infrastructure, healthcare, shopping, and other social aspects have all gone digital. Banks also run their transactions on online platforms.

This high dependency on the Internet should make us question the vulnerability of the information and data we have shared. How easily can critical data be accessed without an authorization? Such a question will automatically lead to putting security measures into place.

Discussed below are some of the data security types that can help protect your sensitive data.

- **Critical Security Infrastructure**

This type of data pertains to the advanced cybersecurity

systems we rely on in modern society. Let us break it further down and mention a few examples of critical infrastructure: traffic lights, shopping centers as well as the electricity grid. Having any of these vital infrastructures makes it an easy target for unauthorized access and cyber-attacks. For instance, an electricity grid can easily be a target of cyber-attacks.

Therefore, companies and organizations whose data involves the critical infrastructure should put measures in place to protect it from getting in the wrong hands. They need to understand the sensitivity of the information they are handling because it is a critical factor in society's well-being.

Additionally, those companies that do not directly deal with critical infrastructure should come with defensive measures to protect it because an attack on could have a significant impact on everyone, including them.

- **The Application Security**

This is one of the must-have data security measures you should consider. It works using the hardware and software techniques to handle impending security threats that can arise towards any sensible data.

Having practical information kept in applications is high risk because they are easily accessible over the Internet, and hackers will access it. Only do so when there are adequate security measures to keep data secured from unauthorized access.

Antivirus programs are some of the application security types. Such protective measures help ensure there is no unauthorized access to data. Additionally, these measures also provide companies that can detect any suspicious activities and puts in place defensive counter attacks.

- **The Network Security**

Having known that data security is more concerned with the threats coming from outside, the network security protects your data from any unauthorized access from people that could have malicious intentions. The network security system keeps data safe by regulating who has access to it and setting security measures; it also detects who has unauthorized access.

With the current technological advances, security measures are getting more sophisticated with the introduction of machine learning to regulate any abnormal traffic as well as detecting threats earlier enough. This type of data protection keeps on implementing procedures and policies that help in preventing unwarranted access and exploitation of data.

Examples of network security implementations include

monitored internet access, strong passwords, and software encryption firewalls.

- **The Cloud Security**

The cloud is a result of competent security measures. This is a kind of data security type that is software-based. It monitors and protects data in the cloud resources. Cloud security companies are consistently implementing and developing new cloud security tools that are playing a pivotal role in securing data.

There is a particular myth associated with cloud computing that it is insecure compared to other data security measures. People think that storing your data manually is more secure because you can control it. Research has, however, revealed that storing data in the cloud is safer than storing it physically in a hard disc. It is also easier to control data stored in the cloud.

In 2018, a research carried out by Alert revealed that data stored on-premise receives an average of 62 attacks while data kept in the cloud experiences an average of 25 attacks.

Storing data in the cloud is more secure, saves you the stress of regularly checking on it, and very affordable. It highly recommended using the cloud as your data storage platform. The future is even bright for cloud security thanks to ongoing technological advancements.

- **The IoT (Internet of Things) Security**

Internet of things refers to various critical cyber-physical elements, including printers, Wi-Fi routers, and CCTV cameras. IoT is a type of data security that focuses more on the networks, consumer devices, and other places where data is stored. There exist a lot of IoT devices that are vulnerable to security breaches. This, therefore, needs severe protective measures from all concerned users.

According to research, security is the biggest reason why enterprises hesitate about buying the Internet of things devices. They fear involving it in their business because sensible data might be accessed by unwarranted personnel.

It, therefore, needs everyone's efforts to come up with measures of how data and information can be secured through the Internet of things. Failure to this, we shall be losing critical information and data to unauthorized people who will ruin it.

If your business is run on online platforms, for instance, someone can hack into your system and get your products for free. They can also take your funds and leave you in a financial crisis. This paints the picture of the importance of data security.

Next, we discuss some of the steps you should take when securing data. Read on to find out!

Securing Data

Data security is vital not only for business establishments but for a regular computer user as well. We have discussed the various ways data is essential to us and why we need to secure it. Losing valuable information like bank account details, payment information, as well as client information, can be very difficult to replace. You can imagine the level of damage that can happen if such information falls into the wrongs hands.

Losing data to natural disasters like fires or floods is crushing and mostly uncontrollable, but losing such sensitive data to malware infections or hackers can result in such dire consequences. The good news, however, is that you can control and prevent cybersecurity attacks. Discussed below are the measures you need to take towards safeguarding your data.

- **Assess the Risks**

Any data security measure begins with assessing the levels of risk available. This goes a long way in helping you identify the possible risks and what can be the case if you lost sensitive data through system crash or malware infections.

Below are other threats you are likely to identify during a risk assessment

- during natural disasters, such as floods, fires, and malicious damage.
- People authorized to have access to data.
- Identify individuals that regularly use the Internet and e-mail systems in which people are allowed to access sensitive data and those who aren't.
- The use of passwords and how you will maintain them.
- Which kind of firewall and malware solutions are you going to use?
- Educate and sensitize people working with you about what they should do when faced with a security breach.

After carefully analyzing the high potential security threats, go ahead and identify more severe risks and prioritize them. It is also advisable to outline a business continuity plan that your team will use in case of a system breakdown. You likewise frequently check security implementations to ensure they meet the standards of your growing business.

- **Secure Your Data**

After carefully assessing the security threats your data is facing, the next thing should be coming up with defensive measures to prevent that from happening. Given the seriousness of the threats sensitive information faces in the modern world, the best step you can take to keep off intruders should involve a combination of advanced technology, physical preventive tools as well as educated staff. Ensure you are operating on well-defined policies and make your staff is aware of them. Highlighted below are some of the steps you can take towards securing data.

Data security is vital not only for business establishments but for a regular computer user as well. We have discussed the various ways data is essential to us and why we need to secure it. Losing valuable information like bank account details, payment information, as well as client information, can be very difficult to replace. You can imagine the level of damage that can happen if such information falls into the wrongs hands

- o Install alarms and monitoring cameras in your data center or office.
- o Don't allow public access to computers that contain manage sensitive data.

o Come up with active security measures that will restrict internet access.

o Always update the anti-malware system. An outdated system is as good as useless.

o Additionally, ensure the operating system is equipped with the latest features.

o Prevent hacking attacks by installing intrusion detecting software.

o Ensure your system has a reliable supply of power.

- **Ensure Mobile Data is Secured**

In today's world, handheld devices have become a popular way of storing data and communication. It is, however, alarming how data is lost through such devices. Handheld devices are very vulnerable to data theft by getting damaged or being stolen. You, therefore, need to put different measures in place to ensure data is secured and safeguarded. Below are some of the things you can do.

o Always back up your data on removable devices and stored on multiple copies.

o Whenever the device is left somewhere, always activate the password protection.

o When you are in a public place, always ensure you don't leave the device in a home, it can be stolen o Mobile devices are very fragile; always ensure you protect them from impending physical damage.

It takes a lot of effort to protect data from attacks and cyber threats. It might be costly in some cases, but it is worth every penny. Losing sensitive data to hackers can be something you will never recover from. To protect your data when you can!

Importance of Data Security

From the beginning of the article up to this point, you are now are aware of the significant data carries and why we should protect it. I believe that it has been well tackled. Next, we discuss the importance of data and why it should be kept from falling in the wrong hands. Below are some of the many essential uses of data.

- **Data is liable**

Those of us in the business industry will understand how data is important to us and what it means by calling it an asset. The information regarding the type of products and services provided is essential. In business, for example, you cannot share your strategic plans with and financial objectives with a competitor, they will use it against you, and you will be on the losing end. Other forms of essential data, like client information, are also something precious. It will cost you a lot when such kind of information is breached and finds its way into the hackers. Not only will the clients sue you, but it will also affect the company's image seriously. You are therefore advised to keep information and data secure using the methods we discussed earlier in this article or risk losing it all. Consequently, it needs everyone's efforts to come up with measures of how data and information can be secured through the Internet of things. Failure to this, we shall be losing critical information and data to unauthorized people who will ruin it.

- **It Maintains the Business Reputation**

Almost all kinds of businesses provide products and services to their customers or rather clients. When a customer walks into your business establishments and buys a product or service using the credit card, they trust you with sensitive information. It is, therefore, up to you to keep such sensitive data secure and prevent it from reaching unauthorized personnel. Any kind of security breach, no matter how small that could lead to leaking of information, can have severe damage to the reputation of your business. The client whose data has been leaked might take legal action against your business and trust me; you won't like the consequences. All firms and companies are, therefore, advised to take data security seriously. It will not only impact your business negatively by tainting its reputation but by making you incur extra costs dealing with court proceedings and other legal actions taken against your business.

Chapter 10:

Types of Cyber-Attacks and How to Prevent Them

In computing, there are situations where sensitive information may face a threat of access by unwanted people. Computers and computer networks are the critical points where these data can be exploited and used for various reasons. People who gain access to this information usually attempt to steal, benefit, destroy, expose, modify, disable, or control. The access is often unauthorized and targets computer infrastructures, networks, information systems, and private data. This way, cyber-attacks can, therefore, be termed as cyber terrorism or cyber warfare undertaken by individuals, groups, organizations, or society.

A cyber-attack is, therefore, deliberate access to unauthorized information of computer networks, systems, and other technological devices by the use of malicious datasets or codes. The outcome is usually a disruption as well as the compromise of the information resulting in loss of essential data and identity theft, among others. Also referred to as computer network attack, cyber-attacks began in the 1980s and rose over the years. However, measures have been implemented, especially in government and institutional data, to ascertain the security of such information. An attacker, in this case, is an individual, group, or the process of data access to restricted information.

The prevalence of cyber-attacks has become rampant in different regions globally with 2017, seeing the rise of up to two billion stolen data accompanied by a ransomware payment reaching two billion US dollars. Some cyberattacks target private devices, therefore, resulting in identity theft, especially for banks and credit cards. Others focus on user sensitive details to access central databases. On the other hand, the world has also experienced global cyber-attacks where viruses have been planted in computers. Individuals behind such attacks often highlight their demands and provide an antivirus after their conditions are met. As such, there have been multiple types of cyberattacks depending on the attacker and specific data under threat.

Types of Cyber Attacks

Denial of service attacks also includes distributed denial of service, is where the attacker targets the resource system of the computer and makes it unresponsive to service requests. However, the distributed denial of service attack originates from different host machines damaged by malicious software from an attacker. This type of cyber-attack does not necessarily provide direct benefits to the attacker. It only stops the whole process, which may become quite beneficial if the system is of a business competitor. Besides, denial of service attacks may come in handy when an attacker wants to launch an attack hence stops the resource system, including securities and firewalls, and commence an attack.

Denial of service attacks may also come in different forms, TCP SYN flood attack, botnets, ping-of-death, smurf, and teardrop. The TCP SYN flood attack is where the attacker targets Transmission Control Protocols when the system is awaiting connections requests in a queue and becomes unresponsive during the initialization of the connection. Teardrop aims the sequential IP packets by making them overlap, therefore confusing the system and causing it to crash. Smurf attacks use IP spoofing while ping of death focuses on IP packets as well. Botnets, on the other hand, are quite different as they involve millions of computers affected by malware, and the hacker can choose which to attack as he or she has control over all the systems.

Malware Attacks

This is another type of cyber-attack consisting of unwanted software being installed into a computer system without the knowledge of the owner. In most cases, the software is established when an individual is online or has a connection where a hacker can gain access to their computers. More so, malware attacks come in different forms based on where it intends to damage. Most of them attach to original codes and propagate to simulate the application or the internet. Common types of malware attacks include macro viruses, file and system infectors, stealth and polymorphic viruses, logic bombs, Trojans, ransomware, worms, and droppers.

Viruses are the most common malware attack depending on how they are meant to infect a given system. Macro viruses are specifically intended to affect computer applications, for example, Microsoft Word and Excel, when initialized. Polymorphic viruses focus on encryptions and decryption, especially when using a decryption program, while stealth viruses are responsible for compromising malware detection applications and conceal the scope of an infected file. File and system infectors comprise cyber-attacks that use a virus to infect specific areas within the computer, such as executable codes of files and records in the hard disk.

Trojans are programs that hide within essential system applications but accompany a malicious function. In this case, Trojans allows a hacker to open and gain access to the necessary files without interacting with securities installed. Worms are also a type of malware attack that is commonly transferred by email attachments and activated once the mail is opened. Droppers are another form of malware but used to spread and hide viruses making scanning processes difficult to identify malware. Ransomware is the most dangerous type of malware as it blocks the user from accessing information; therefore, it may be used as a threat to specific demands to be met.

Eavesdropping Attacks

These are cyber-attacks which occur when an attacker intercepts network traffic and gain access to crucial data such as passwords and other confidential information transferred through the connection. Researchers have categorized eavesdropping into two, active, and passive eavesdropping. Passive eavesdropping entails an attacker monitoring and listening to the message being transferred and learning about it. Active eavesdropping involves a hacker physical disguising as a beneficial party to the user by requesting the message to the transmitter in a process refers to as probing or scanning. Passive eavesdropping is the most dangerous form as they often go unnoticed when compared to active eavesdropping. The best technique to use to avoid eavesdropping attacks is through data encryption.

Cross-Site Scripting Attacks

In some cases, an attacker may use cross-site scripting to gain access to sensitive data through thirty party web resources. That is, the attacker first establishes the targeted information or system and introduces contents consisting of malicious JavaScript in the website database. This malicious program will remain in the database until when the victim opts to requests the webpage. The website will accompany the content with the page embedded within the HTML body to the browser of the victim. When the page completes loading, the malicious script will execute, allowing the attacker to gain access to the computer.

In some instances, the hacker may choose to accompany other vulnerabilities that provide more loopholes to access different areas of your computer. The hacker will then be able to collect all the information needed, including controlling the machine. Cross-site scripting may take various forms, but JavaScript is the most supported and standard used on the web today. Cross-site scripting can, however, affected not only one victim, but also affect others who load similar websites. As to avoid this type of cyber-attack, ensure all the web information is first filtered and validated as well as preventing sending specific information to the resource. Besides, you can disable client-side scripting, making the user have control of the information shared through the web resources.

Password Attacks

Passwords are the most common attacks experienced by

victims as they are the sole mechanisms to authenticate the access of user data in specific areas. Acquiring someone's password is most preferably when peeking on their devices or ATMs or other peeks. However, this is not cyber-attacks, as hackers usually gain access to the computer and collect these passwords to open private accounts through computer connections. Like most cyberattacks, password attacks come in different forms and include decryption of passwords, gaining access to the database, outright guessing, and through social engineering.

One of the most common is brute-force password access, which is the guessing of different possible potential words or numbers used as passwords with the intention of one being correct. Another form is through a dictionary attack where a hacker tries to gain access to the connection and computer, and copy the encrypted file and compare it to the dictionary with a similar and possible password format. Some may go ahead and decrypt the password and gain access. One of the primary countermeasures to avoid password attacks is by introducing an account lockout policy that automatically locks after specific password attempts.

Drive-By Attack

These are another common type of cyber-attack where an

attacker can readily spread malware through insecure websites. That is, they quickly install malicious script in HTTP or PHP codes in one or more webpages targeting victims who visit these sites. Drive-by scripts may either install the malware into the victim's computer directly or redirect them to the websites of the hacker. In this case, the malware can download immediately the web is loaded or visiting a given website or pop-up pages. This type of cyber-attack does not rely on the user clicking anything or accepting any downloads. This will then enable an attacker to infect your computer without your consent.

When installed into your system, drive-by attacks may infect a program, the operating system as a whole, or browser with security issues. The primary solution for this type of cyber-attack is to keep your computer browser, operating system, and applications updated. You can as well stay away from websites that look suspicious or possess malicious codes essential for causing infections. However, understand that any website can be hacked and compromise the security of your computer. More so, remove any unnecessary or excess applications and programs as they make your device more vulnerable to threats. In other words, the more plugins you have, the more susceptible you are to drive-by cyber-attacks.

Phishing Attacks

Phishing and spear-phishing is the process of sending emails to victims with the aim of gaining access to their personal information or persuade them to do something. The emails are often fake but seem genuine and accompany malware, which quickly loads into your system when you open the attachment. Some useful links to certain websites that lure you into following the instructions given and ending up submitting private data to attackers. The trickery used generally combines social engineering and related techniques to ensure the victim is well influenced to accept to the terms highlighted. Attackers usually have a deeper understanding of their victims, therefore, creating content which suits their personality and relevance.

Identifying these forms of cyberattacks is ordinarily tricky to victims, henceforth finding it hard to defend or resist from handing over crucial data, primarily when a hacker uses email spoofing. Others use website cloning, which commonly fools victims to believe that the emails are legitimate and from trusted sources. There are several ways to reduce and protect yourself from phishing attacks, and one of them is through the use of critical thinking by taking the time to read through and understanding about the sender. Another form is by hovering on the link by deciphering the URL and understands it but never click at first. You can also analyze the headers by learning about the domain and by sandboxing to try and figure out the legitimacy of the mail.

Man-In-The-Middle Attacks

Man-in-the-middle cyber-attacks occur when an attacker gets access between the connection of the victim and server. This type also comes in different forms, which are session hijacking, IP spoofing, and replays. IP spoofing is where the attacker convinces your computer that it is communicating with a genuine entity, therefore, allowing for the access. Similarly, the attacker sends packets with IP source resembling the host instead of the original IP source address making its accept it and act on it. A replay attack is when the attacker impersonates the victim by saving old messages and sending them sooner after the interception. Replays are, however, not valid to hackers as victims can readily prevent them through nonce and timestamps.

Session hijacking is where the attacker intervenes in a session of trusted clients and servers while the primary IP address is substituted, and the server continues with the session. The client first connects to the server, and when the hijacking happens, the attacker gains control by disconnecting the server the client. It then replaces the IP address and continues the sessions with the server as well as the client. With limited countermeasures to man-in-the-middles cyber-attacks, data encryption, and the use of digital certificates may play a significant role in preventing these threats. You should know it is always challenging to understand when an attacker is within a given service; therefore, crucial to forever remain protected against man-in-the-middle cyber-attacks.

SQL Injection Attack

This is a driven-database website attack that occurs when an attacker runs a SQL query within a specific database through the data inputs of a client. The commands are injected in data-planes to execute predefined SQL instructions. When injected successfully, SQL queries access confidential and other sensitive information from the database enabling the attacker to perform the intended purpose. In this case, the data becomes open to the attacker who then can read, change, execute operations, copy, recover and issue commands within the operating system.

For example, a website form may require a user's account name or password, which can be readily be pulled from the database. When such individuals use SQL injections successfully, it allows the information to be drawn from the database and delivered to the attacker at an instant as it already has the details from the victim. The vulnerabilities typically arise due to SQL lacking the ability to differentiate between controls and data planes, thus essential for dynamic SQL, PHP, and ASP. As to protect yourself from this type of cyber-attack, use the least privilege model, which facilitates permissions in your database. This model allows for stable codes that only validate input data of applications through stored procedures and prepared statements.

How to Prevent Cyber Attacks

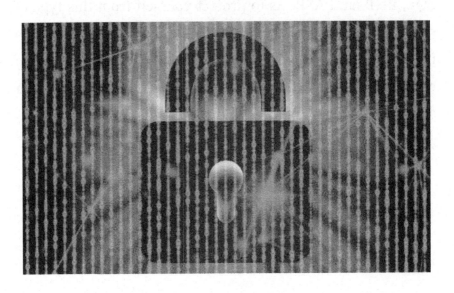

- **Limit Individuals Accessing Your System**

As already mentioned, among the primary causes of cyberattacks is public use of computer networks and the sharing of communication devices. This has been found to contribute to cyber threats and attacks commonly happening today. As to cub this, you can begin by limiting the number of people accessing your system, especially strangers and uninvited people. You can achieve this by securing your computers by updating software and the use of antiviruses as well as updating the operating system. You can again use company-approved programs and applications rather than purchasing from third parties. This method of prevention is quite useful, especially when you have doubts about people and sources, which tend to cause a threat to your files.

- **Learn About Cyber Attacks**

You can never begin protecting yourself from something you have no idea about how it works; therefore, the need to learn the basics. One of the best ways to do this is through learning about cyber-attacks and become aware of how they operate and harm computers. Having a general knowledge enables you to figure out ways of handling threats and the accompanying attacks when they happen as well as the mitigation measures. This will hence provide exceptional results, especially when you receive emails that you have no idea what they are and go ahead understanding instead of clicking every link you see. Search about facts and continually gain more knowledge with time as attackers also change their tactics over time.

- **Regulate System Infiltration**

Malware is common, and sometimes avoiding them may become a challenge; therefore, continually infect more computers globally. However, you can prevent this type of cyber-attack by readily regulating infiltrations by malware. As to achieve this, ensure any device inserted in your computer is free from any malware such as viruses. You can check it while offline to avoid spreading it through your network. Also, ensure that no third party accesses your computer and enters unknown data as some may plant-specific instructions that allow them to control your system remotely.

- **Enhance Physical Protection**

Other than focusing on online, computer programs, and application security, you should also put in mind the protection of the physical computer itself. Begin by having a lengthy and robust password of not less than eight characters with a mixture of lower and upper letters as well as numbers and symbols. Use identity card authentications where the need is to ascertain your data, especially when providing security to confidential information. Keep all these securities protected at all times without having vulnerabilities that may compromise your cyber-attack security measures.

- **Ghettoize Networks**

Another primary source of computer cyber-attack is through the network, which connects different devices to the server. The host typically has limited threats to your system, but third parties, which are hackers, in this case, may use your connection as an entry point to access your data. Then you have to conceal these loopholes as they contribute to threats of cyber-attacks. One of the practices to do is to prevent other people's devices from accessing private networks by securing stations that facilitate file sharing. Another form is through becoming very cautious, especially on what you share online, as some information you share may be used against you. Besides, ensure that you avoid using public networks with devices that consist of critical and sensitive data as most hackers may take advantage and benefit from your mistake.

- **Constantly Update Your Securities**

Most often, the best way to prevent cyber-attacks is to ensure that your system is full of all applications, software, and programs that facilitate the needed protection. What many fail to understand is that cyber-attacks, especially for malware change over time, and if you fail to make an update, your securities may fail to protect the system. In this case, the best way to handle these attracts is by ensuring that antiviruses, antispyware, firewalls, and software in the operating system are updated. Make these updates regularly to ensure you have the more recent version of your securities. You should be aware that hackers also understand this, and any delays in making updates may cost you. As such, ensure that you quickly make the updates as soon as they are available.

Made in the USA
Coppell, TX
06 January 2020

14138434R00115